NATIONAL DEFENSE ᴿᴱᶜᵉ  E

T0096280

Assessment of the Politico-Military Campaign to Counter ISIL and Options for Adaptation

Linda Robinson

Prepared for the Office of the Secretary of Defense

For more information on this publication, visit www.rand.org/t/RR1290

Library of Congress Cataloging-in-Publication Data
is available for this publication.

ISBN: 978-0-8330-9482-7

Published by the RAND Corporation, Santa Monica, Calif.
© Copyright 2016 RAND Corporation
RAND® is a registered trademark.

Support RAND
Make a tax-deductible charitable contribution at
www.rand.org/giving/contribute

www.rand.org

Preface

The attacks by Islamic State in Iraq and the Levant (ISIL) in Paris on November 13, 2015, represented a watershed moment that spurred wide international recognition of the growth and reach of ISIL and a resulting consensus that more active measures were needed to confront the group. The counter-ISIL campaign has accelerated since the fall of 2015, but questions persist as to the exact suite of measures needed and the adequacy of the overall strategy to degrade and defeat ISIL. These questions also grew more acute with Russia's military intervention on behalf of the Syrian regime starting September 30, 2015, which greatly strengthened the regime's faltering hand against its armed opponents. The anti-ISIL fight in that country has increasingly blended with that civil war, as ISIL moved westward and a skittish Turkey sought to preserve room for opposition Arab forces against the Syrian Kurds.

This report assesses the first 18 months of the campaign to counter ISIL. This analysis should be of interest to the policymakers and legislators charged with overseeing the counter-ISIL strategy, as well as the military and civilian practitioners involved in executing it. The paper evaluates the viability of the partnered approach by evaluating the capabilities and interests of the various forces that the United States is attempting to support, considers the political impediments to achieving the stated objective of defeating ISIL, and assesses the approach compared with other potential alternatives. This report recommends steps to (1) improve the partnered approach to the military campaign, (2) formulate a detailed approach to the foundational political line of effort, and (3) synchronize the political and military elements of the strategy so these lines of effort effectively enable one another.

In late 2015, the U.S. government decided to deploy an expeditionary targeting force aimed at gaining intelligence and targeting top ISIL leaders, and this effort yielded numerous results in the first months of 2016. The accelerating campaign against the ISIL leadership raised the prospect that this important line of effort might outrun the advances in building a competent and coherent hold force in both Iraq and Syria. Similarly, the advances on this front cast into relief the absence of the necessary political agreements in Iraq and Syria to assure that new terrorist and insurgent activity would not emerge to fill the vacuum left by ISIL's demise.

The research was conducted within the International Security and Defense Policy Center of the RAND National Defense Research Institute, a federally funded research and development center sponsored by the Office of the Secretary of Defense, the Joint Staff, the Unified Combatant Commands, the Navy, the Marine Corps, the defense agencies, and the defense Intelligence Community. The views expressed in this report are those of the author and do not reflect the official policy or position of the Department of Defense or the U.S. Government.

For more information on the International Security and Defense Policy Center, see www.rand.org/nsrd/ndri/centers/isdp.html or contact the director (contact information is provided on web page).

Contents

Figure and Table

Figure

Table

Acknowledgments

The author wishes to thank Seth G. Jones, director of RAND's International Security and Defense Program; Charles Ries, vice president, International, at RAND; and Jim Dobbins, RAND senior fellow, for comments on drafts of this report and discussions about events in Iraq and Syria. In addition, Michael O'Hanlon of the Brookings Institution and Douglas Ollivant, a RAND adjunct fellow, served as peer reviewers and provided thoughtful comments and suggestions that greatly improved this document. RAND research associate Madeline Magnuson and project associate Anthony Atler provided valuable research support for this effort. The author is also indebted to RAND communications analysts Erin Dick and James Chiesa, administrative assistant Lovancy Ingram, production editor Julienne Amsden, and research editor Linda Theung for superb editorial assistance. Many individuals in Iraq, Jordan, and Kuwait, as well as the United States, generously shared their insights and provided unclassified information for use in this report. This report results from a RAND-sponsored research program. Comments or questions should be addressed to the author, Linda Robinson, RAND senior international policy analyst, at linda_robinson@rand.org.

Abbreviations

AAH	Asa'ib Ahl al-Haq
ANF	al-Nusra Front
CTS	Counter Terrorism Service
DoD	U.S. Department of Defense
FSA	Free Syrian Army
HMMWV	high-mobility multipurpose wheeled vehicle
IED	improvised explosive device
ISF	Iraqi Security Forces
ISIL	Islamic State of Iraq and the Levant
ISR	intelligence, surveillance, and reconnaissance
KH	Kata'ib Hizballah
KSF	Kurdish Security Forces
MFF	Mosul Fighting Forces
NATO	North Atlantic Treaty Organization
NSF	New Syrian Forces
PKK	Kurdish Workers' Party
PMF	Popular Mobilization Forces
SDF	Syrian Democratic Forces
SOF	Special Operations Forces
TOW	tube-launched, optically tracked, wireless-guided
YPG	Syrian Kurdish People's Defense Units (Kurdish *Yekineyen Parastina Gel*)

CHAPTER ONE

Introduction

This report assesses the prospects of success in countering the Islamic State of Iraq and the Levant (ISIL) through a partner-based strategy.[1] This in-depth analysis of the capabilities, limitations, and intentions of the anti-ISIL forces, as well as measures that the United States and the coalition have taken to date to support them, finds that the ways and means employed over the first year of the campaign were insufficient. The U.S. administration tacitly recognized this in the summer of 2015 and began to develop options for accelerating its campaign. ISIL's attacks in Paris in November 2015, followed by attacks in Brussels in March 2016, served as a wake-up call about the magnitude of the threat, as it demonstrated ISIL's ability to reach well beyond the borders of its declared caliphate in Iraq and Syria. The growth of ISIL extended to eight recognized affiliates outside the core territory and a worldwide network that had funneled more than 38,000 foreign fighters into Iraq, Syria, and, more recently, to its main external affiliate in Libya.

U.S. Secretary of Defense Ashton Carter has argued that Iraq and Syria, as the core of ISIL's declared caliphate, must remain the focus of effort. The rationale is that ISIL's control of a large, contiguous swath of territory in Iraq and Syria enables the group to operate as a proto-

---

[1] This paper uses the term *Islamic State of Iraq and the Levant (ISIL)* because it is the term employed by the U.S. government as established by the National Counter-Terrorism Center. Other terms in wide usage include the *Islamic State*, the *Islamic State of Iraq and al-Sham*, and *Dai'ish* (a mildly derogatory acronym based on the Arabic transliterated name, *al-Dawla al-Islamiya fi Iraq wa al-Sham*).

state, which attracts attention and recruits, inspires attacks by affiliated groups and individuals, and may serve as a launching pad for future attacks outside the region. According to this analysis, ISIL's base in Iraq and Syria serves as the engine for its worldwide network and web of affiliates.

The U.S. strategy to degrade and defeat ISIL relies heavily on effective partner forces to combat the group and to clear and hold the extensive territory it has seized in Iraq and Syria. This reliance on partner forces reflects the emphasis that the U.S. national military strategy places on effective partnerships around the world as a way to safeguard U.S. national security interests. The rationale for this pillar of the strategy is that only effective and competent indigenous forces can hold terrain permanently with the backing of the population. This report focuses on the manner in which the partnered approach was implemented in the first 18 months of the campaign. The Iraqi government and the moderate Syrian opposition both seek support from the United States. Yet military and political factors make applying this approach in Iraq and Syria extremely challenging. The Iraqi Security Forces (ISF), the army in particular, remains weak, while the motivated and well-equipped Shia militias are feared by many Sunnis. The Iraqi government remains ambivalent about arming Sunnis to fight against ISIL. In Syria, most of the armed groups are primarily concerned with ousting President Bashar al-Assad, and frictions impede cooperation among opposition groups.

Outside actors with diverse interests further complicate the picture. Most notably, Iran plays a significant competing military and political role in supporting the Iraqi government, the Assad regime, and an array of militias that are a major force in Iraq and Syria. Other countries, including those that are coalition partners with the United States, are supporting Islamist anti-Assad forces that the United States opposes.

Thus, the United States faces a contest for influence in the region. Iran's enormous influence in Iraq is not likely to wane, at least while the ISIL threat to Iraq remains existential, and, in any event, many of Iran's deeply rooted alliances with Iraq's Shia majority will persist. Yet Iraq's government has urgently sought assistance from the U.S. government for material reasons and to counterbalance Iran's influence.[2] While Iraqi national identity has been in flux given the sea change from Sunni to Shia dominance since 2003, Iraqi nationalism may well reassert itself vis-à-vis Iran and lead to strengthened U.S.-Iraqi ties in the future.[3] The recent demonstrations in Iraq notably featured nonsectarian calls for better government and aggressive measures to halt corruption, to which the government responded with numerous reforms and reducing the number of ministries and patronage positions.

In Syria, the situation is far more complex. The advances of ISIL and other extremist forces have weakened the Assad regime, which in turn have prompted Russia and Iran to increase their support for Syria. Beginning in September 2015, Russia dramatically stepped up its support to the Assad regime with airstrikes aimed primarily at non-

---

[2]   In a public appearance at the Center for Strategic and International Studies on April 16, 2015, Iraqi Prime Minister Haider al-Abadi asked for continued U.S. military and intelligence support and made the following statement about Iran's military role in Iraq:

> I've told my Iranian friends very bluntly they are helping Iraq, thank you very much, but everything must be done through the government of Iraq. Any other way they are doing it, I consider it and my government considers as hostile to Iraq. And they claim they're not doing it outside the government; they're doing it through the government. . . . Iraqi sovereignty is of utmost importance. And I think many of the political blocs are with me on this and the religious leadership in Najaf was very, very clear about this. Iraqi sovereignty must be respected. Although we welcome any help that's given to us, but it shouldn't trespass and shouldn't break the Iraqi sovereignty. And that's our position with the Iranians (Haider al-Abadi, transcript of interview in a public forum with Dr. Jon B. Alterman, senior vice president, Zbigniew Brzezinski, chair in Global Security and Geostrategy, and director, Center for Strategic and International Studies, *Statesmen's Forum: Looking Forward: A Holistic Strategy for Iraq*, Washington, D.C.: Superior Transcripts LLC, April 16, 2015).

[3]   Haddad argued that "the Iraqi nation-state is an entity subscribed to by the overwhelming majority of Arab Iraqis" and that "sectarian relations are dynamic and are dictated by the constantly advancing and receding salience of sectarian identities in relation to Iraqi national identity." (Fanar Haddad, *Sectarianism in Iraq: Antagonistic Visions of Unity*, New York: Columbia University Press, 2011, pp. 206, 208.) After the 2006–2007 civil war, sectarian tensions receded, but they have returned with several actions against Sunnis by the Maliki government and the rise of ISIL. Iraqi national identity, if the country survives, would have to be one that recognizes the Shia majority in contrast to the Sunni-Baathist version of national identity. But the deep mistrust between the two communities may prevent the formation of a common narrative, as Haddad notes: "Sunni identity today carries a victimhood complex rivaling that of the Shi'a" (Haddad, 2011, p. 209).

ISIL opponents of the regime, apparently aiming to help Assad regain territory and solidify control of an area stretching from Damascus to the Mediterranean coast, where Russia has a naval base and many of Assad's Alawite constituents reside. The significant infusion of four dozen Russian military fighter jets and helicopters—as well as air defense, artillery, and rocket systems—suggested a sustained military effort to shore up the faltering Assad regime.

Syrian Kurds made significant headway against ISIL strongholds, but, as with the Iraqi Kurds, their reach in Syria's Arab areas may be limited. In addition, their advances prompted a severe reaction from Turkey, which faces its own internal Kurdish terrorist group allied with the Syrians. A U.S. military program to train and equip Syrian fighters found few recruits and faltered once fielded, leading the administration to suspend the program in October 2015. The success of the U.S. strategy relies on friendly forces to take and hold territory. The obvious way to harness the energies of more local partners against ISIL would be to embrace their fight against Assad, rather than continue what appears to be a fruitless effort to persuade Syrian to attack only ISIL, which has not been a major player in the populated western part of the country. Yet among the risks of a more-robust U.S. effort in Syria is the prospect that Syria, Russia, or Iran could retaliate against coalition aircraft currently targeting ISIL in Syrian territory or U.S. forces in Iraq.[4]

Russian actions have posed a stark dilemma for the United States. The United States likely would lose all credibility with Syrian opposition forces, as well as its regional allies, if it were to join forces with Russia to shore up Assad; such a bargain to gain their support to fight ISIL would be Faustian indeed. Even standing by while Russian strikes decimate groups supported by the United States damages U.S. credibility. Russia's bold gambit challenges the United States, but also presents an opportunity for the United States to come together with North Atlantic Treaty Organization (NATO) and regional allies, as well

---

[4]   Karl P. Mueller, Jeffrey Martini, and Thomas Hamilton, *Airpower Options for Syria: Assessing Objectives and Missions for Aerial Intervention*, Santa Monica, Calif.: RAND Corporation, RR-446-CMEPP, 2013. This RAND report provides a detailed analysis of the air options in Syria. Although written in 2013, the technical analysis remains relevant.

as the internal Syrian opposition, to reject Russia's attempt to shore up Assad and forge a basic but substantive consensus on the need to fight ISIL and achieve a transitional Syrian government. To be credible, such an effort would need to create new facts on the ground and recognize that the Syrian population principally cares about the fight to remove Assad. To gain the support of regional allies and Syrians, the United States would need to back their fight against Assad while still pushing for a negotiated solution. A simultaneous campaign to defeat ISIL and put sufficient military pressure on the regime to negotiate Assad's departure would represent a significantly increased U.S. commitment. Strengthening a moderate opposition coalition that may include Islamists but exclude al Qaeda affiliates could create the conditions, including a sufficiently robust indigenous ground force, for lasting defeat of ISIL and, if it held together, stabilization of the territory in the longer term. Taking this path would require acknowledging not only the reality of a two-front war in Syria, but the merging of the two wars and the basic need for a ground force of Syrians to reclaim their country, if it is indeed to be saved. The current relative division of labor might be maintained, wherein the United States supports other countries that would lead the anti-Assad fight while retaining its leading role in the anti-ISIL fight. But a basic understanding as to the requirements, goals, and composition of the alliance would need to be clarified.

Successfully implementing a partnered approach to counter ISIL must take into account all of these complexities. Given the number of difficulties and weaknesses of the various partners, this analysis suggests that a minimalist approach to partnering will not likely yield sufficient results. The fundamental premise does seem sound: That the only way to gain lasting defeat of ISIL—which has become in effect a land-holding proto-state—is through ground forces that can take and hold territory. The weaknesses and limitations of the available partners can only be overcome through more-robust support and a greater effort to coordinate among them. Given the urgent need to arrest ISIL's momentum, the United States is forced to choose the best of the available options and mitigate the negative effects. The need to achieve short-term results will have to be balanced with a longer-term program to achieve regional stability.

The principal alternatives to this partnered approach are either a large-scale U.S. military intervention involving tens of thousands of U.S. combat troops or containment to limit spillover and shore up regional allies. The costs and long-term risks of both these alternatives suggest that increased effort to make the partnered approach work is warranted. Direct U.S. military intervention would be long, costly, and unpopular at home and in the region, and ultimately might fail to defeat the threat if the presence of tens of thousands of U.S. combat troops incited an unending stream of recruits to the ISIL cause. Containment would be much less costly and would avoid the risks of large-scale ground force intervention, but the porous borders and unconventional nature of the threat would make this approach difficult to implement—as the Paris attacks sadly illustrated. Containment would also leave the Iraqi government highly dependent on Iran to support its military operations, which would act as a further accelerant to sectarian conflict. The principal risks of the containment approach are that ISIL would continue to hold large amounts of territory and to expand internationally through affiliates, orchestrated or inspired attacks, and ongoing recruitment on a massive scale. On balance, therefore, the partnered approach appears to combine the least risk with the greatest chance of success.

Objectives, Approach, and Organization

This report examines the current U.S. strategy to counter ISIL and the first 18 months of its implementation. The research objectives are to evaluate the U.S. approach, which relies on a partner-based strategy to take and hold territory, and determine the requirements for successful implementation. The report also evaluates the potential risks and benefits of the current U.S. approach compared with two other approaches: large-scale U.S. combat intervention and containment. The report concludes with recommendations for improvement of the military line of effort and the overall strategy.

This inquiry explores the following questions: What have been the results of the strategy in its first 18 months of implementation? How capable are the military forces countering ISIL? What are the principal gaps in capability that the United States or other partners need to fill in order to achieve a successful counteroffensive? What are the political intentions and conflicting interests that impede a successful counteroffensive? What shortcomings exist in the overall conception or implementation of the current strategy? Are other approaches more likely to succeed at lower cost and/or lower risk? What measures might produce greater results in the near term?

To tackle these questions, the author employed an empirical and inductive method to review and evaluate the most authoritative and current sources of information available. An extensive review of publicly available primary and secondary documents was also conducted. To supplement this document and literature review, the author held discussions with policymakers, as well as those involved in the strategy's implementation; visited sites in Iraq, Jordan, and Kuwait; and held discussions with and received briefings from U.S., coalition, and Iraqi officials, as well as Iraqi citizens. Research for this report was conducted during trips to Iraq, Jordan, and Kuwait in 2015, and through discussions with approximately 200 U.S., coalition, and Iraqi and regional military, as well as civilian officials, experts, and Iraqis displaced by ISIL.[5]

---

[5] In addition to a range of Iraqi and Syrian individuals and academic experts, the author benefited from the perspectives of officials in the Iraqi government; the U.S. Department of State; the Embassies of the United States in Baghdad, Iraq, and Amman, Jordan; the National Security Council staff; the National Counter-Terrorism Center; the Central Intelligence Agency; various elements of the Department of Defense (DoD), including the offices of Middle East Policy and Special Operations/Low-Intensity Conflict; the Joint Chiefs of Staff; the Joint Special Operations Command; the Joint Special Operations Command Center for Counter-Terrorism Studies; the U.S. Special Operations Command–Central Command; the Combined Joint Task Force–Operation Inherent Resolve; subordinate command echelons, including Coalition Forces Land Component Command-Iraq (CFLCC-I), Special Operations Joint Task Force-Iraq (SOJTF-I), Combined Joint Special Operations Task Force-Iraq (CJSOTF-I), and Task Force Panther; the Iraq Counter-Terrorism Service; and other Iraqi commands.

The first step of the inquiry was to review U.S. strategy and its nine lines of effort and assess the implementation of the policy over the past year. Because of the time available to conduct the study, the focus of inquiry was limited to the political and military lines of effort, which bear directly on the partnered strategy to defeat ISIL in Iraq and Syria. In addition to reviewing the strategy documents, the author reviewed the extensive congressional testimony, speeches, and briefings offered by multiple U.S. officials in 2014–2015. The author met with U.S. policy officials at the National Security Council, the State Department, the Department of Defense (DoD), and various intelligence entities, as well as senior Iraqi officials. The assessment of ISIL's objectives, capabilities, and operational effects in Iraq and Syria in 2014–2015 relied on a review of its own literature, including *Dabiq* magazine, statements by ISIL leadership and fighters collected and translated by SITE Intel Group, and conversations with a wide variety of intelligence analysts in the United States and throughout the ISIL-affected region. Recent books by Jessica Stern, William McCants and Michael Weiss provided useful background on ISIL intentions and methods.[6]

Data on the various anti-ISIL forces was gathered on visits to various training sites and commands. Various individuals and officials at coalition and Iraqi commands, as well as the Office of Security Cooperation at the U.S. Embassy in Baghdad, provided unclassified briefings and shared perspectives on the capabilities of Iraqi forces. In addition, U.S. officials discussed the program to train and equip Syrian opposition forces in several locations in the region. The author was invited to the coalition conference in February 2015. Discussions with commanders and staff were held within the Combined Joint Task Force—Operation Inherent Resolve, Combined Forces Land Component Command, Special Operations Joint Task Force, Special Operations Command Central, Combined Joint Special Operations Task Force, and subordinate elements throughout Baghdad and Irbil. Per-

---

6   William McCants, *The ISIS Apocalypse: The History, Strategy and Doomsday Vision of the Islamic State*, New York: St. Martin's Press, 2015; Jessica Stern and J. M. Berger, *ISIS: The State of Terror*, New York: Ecco, 2015; Michael Weiss and Hassan Hassan, *ISIS: Inside the Army of Terror*, New York: Regan Arts, 2015.

sonnel assigned to the U.S. Embassy in Jordan also provided perspectives. U.S. Central Command provided a daily compilation of translated Iraqi, Syrian, and other regional media and social media reports, which provided a primary means of tracking battlefield actions of ISIL and anti-ISIL forces.

The description and analysis of the strengths and weaknesses of the various anti-ISIL forces is followed by an analysis of the measures that the U.S.-led coalition has taken to support them through training, equipment, advisory assistance, and an air campaign. Several capability gaps are identified in areas that include fires, intelligence, logistical support, and leadership, as well as lack of coordination among disparate regular and irregular forces. The subsequent analysis identifies priority areas for addressing military and overall strategic shortfalls. The final section weighs the risks and benefits of adopting a more-robust form of the current partnered strategy, along with a prioritization of diplomatic and military initiatives in Syria, compared with two alternatives.

Several limitations affect the analysis of the capabilities and intentions of both ISIL and the array of anti-ISIL forces. Most obviously, the dynamic nature of the war posed the challenge of analyzing the constant stream of new data on battlefield actions and statements by various actors, including Turkey and other coalition partners. The irregular and clandestine nature of the adversary also presented challenges. While ISIL has openly broadcast its strategic objectives of establishing an Islamic caliphate, instituting its version of Islamic governance, and continuing to expand its territory, its operational and tactical objectives—as well as the composition of its leadership, ranks, and capabilities as a hybrid military force—have only been revealed over time in the course of its actions. Moreover, as ISIL shifted from a form of maneuver warfare to more concealed guerrilla forms of warfare, its intentions and capabilities became harder to discern.

Similarly, the dissolution of a large part of the formal ISF and the multiplication of irregular militia forces in Iraq and Syria complicate the effort to assemble a picture of fighting forces, including their capabilities and intentions. Even for regular units, estimates of forces present for duty and equipment fielded are only approximate, although the U.S.-backed coalition has gained increased understanding of forces operating in Iraq over the past year. The irregular forces' differing political objectives are described chiefly through reliance on their principal leaders' statements, though variances with observed or reported actions are also noted. The assessments of actors' core interests and those issues on which compromise or coordination might be possible are admittedly speculative, but have been grounded in the analysis of their past and recent behavior and statements. Finally, it should be noted that this six-month research project timeline did not permit an exhaustive mapping of the many political factors that complicate a partnered approach to include intra-Shia competition in Iraq, the robust role of Iran, the relatively thin support provided by other Arab countries, and the conflicting aims of Turkey.

The remainder of this report is organized in four chapters: Chapter Two provides background on the counter-ISIL strategy, the political context in Iraq and Syria, and chief characteristics of ISIL. Chapter Three provides an analysis of the strengths, weaknesses, and primary interests of the principal Iraqi and Syrian anti-ISIL forces. Chapter Four reviews the efforts in 2015 undertaken by the U.S.-led coalition in the military and political lines of effort. Chapter Five provides recommendations for improving the military effort and the overall approach.

Principal Recommendations

The following detailed recommendations are aimed at moving the strategy forward from simply degrading ISIL to achieving its lasting defeat in its core territory in Iraq and Syria and thus sapping momentum from its worldwide pretensions. These steps fall into three basic categories of objectives: (1) improve the partnered approach to the military campaign, (2) increase emphasis on the political line of effort, and (3) create greater synchronization of the political and military elements of the strategy. There is an important temporal requirement for this strategy to succeed. Even as the campaign achieves significant progress in capturing or killing ISIL leadership, it must simultaneously build partner capacity and achieve progress on the political front in both countries. Otherwise, the effort runs a high risk of creating a vacuum into which new threat groups will flow. In the case of Syria, the regime's moves to target ISIL with Russia's help may only spur greater recruitment flows to the al Qaeda affiliate, al-Nusra Front (ANF), and its allies.

Both positive and negative developments warrant elevating the counter-ISIL campaign to a higher priority to seize opportunities, gain momentum, and overcome impediments. U.S. efforts cannot entirely compensate for the weaknesses and limitations of partners, but without a greater effort, the strategy runs a significant risk of failure. The anti-ISIL groups have achieved greater gains when united than when uncoordinated or, worse yet, fighting among themselves. Syria should be elevated to an equal priority with Iraq to capitalize on opportunities there and place greater pressure on ISIL activities in Iraq, but the fragmentation of opposition groups greatly decreases the effects of U.S. and allied aid and support. Nonetheless, the entry of Turkey, the United Kingdom, and France into the air war on ISIL in Syria created new prospects for progress on the battlefield and diplomatically. Russian military support to Assad also created an opportunity to rally an international coalition and Syrian opponents behind a renewed attempt to fashion a political transition to a post-Assad regime rather than bow to an indefinitely extended tenure for Assad. The regime lacks a solid indigenous ground force on which it can rely, and there are limits to the ground forces that other countries are likely to send on Assad's behalf.

In Iraq, specific recommendations include:

- Mount an advisory effort that is more robust, empowered, and geographically distributed to include advisers at the tactical level with trusted units, such as the Counter-Terrorism Service (CTS), as well as all area commands in the conflict zone. Several thousand additional personnel would be required to provide force protection, medical evacuation, and counterintelligence.
- Expedite delivery of urgently needed equipment for the ISF, including CTS urgent needs.

- Establish an unconventional warfare program to leverage Sunni tribes' popular rejection of ISIL, gather intelligence, and conduct psychological warfare and sabotage against ISIL forces.
- Commit to funding a long-term train-and-equip program for ISF to include police and national guard (if formed), conditioned on a reciprocal commitment to incorporate proportionate numbers of Sunnis and to transition all militia forces in accordance with the Iraqi constitution.
- Offer robust, high-visibility support to the Iraqi government's program of reforms and decentralization efforts to enable it to achieve concrete progress toward satisfying legitimate demands of the Sunni minority and resolve funding disputes with the Kurdistan Regional Government.

In Syria, specific recommendations include:

- Reenergize diplomatic efforts to seek a transitional regime in Syria in concert with NATO and regional allies, while forging a common strategy among those allies to increase military pressure on the Assad regime and to protect moderate Syrian opposition forces from Russian airstrikes. Russian actions create an opportunity for a new consensus among anti-Assad forces. A united front may eventually persuade Russia and Iran that the costs of sustaining the Assad regime will only continue to mount, and that their interests are better served by supporting a political transition.
- To empower the search for a negotiated solution, assist or support other countries' assistance to Syrian opposition groups that are not affiliated with al Qaeda and adopt less-constrained vetting criteria for Syrian opposition fighters that accepts their interest in fighting the Assad regime. This support should, at a minimum, include antitank and antiaircraft missiles if the coalition is unwilling to provide air support to protect the forces from Russian airstrikes. Such aid is necessary to create negotiating incentives for the Syrian regime.

- Encourage Syrian opposition forces to unite to attack ISIL as part of their offensive, providing additional support to those groups that do so.

In both countries, the following steps could enhance the effectiveness of the air campaign:

- Increase intelligence, surveillance, and reconnaissance (ISR) assets and emphasize an intelligence-driven air campaign while continuing to avoid civilian casualties.
- Increase the speed of the targeting process by delegating target-engagement authority to additional subordinate commands, enabling Iraqi and Syrian forward observers through better equipment and training, and selective use of U.S. joint terminal air controllers.
- The overall strategy can be improved by the following measures:
- Conduct a comprehensive review of the strategy to understand the drivers of the ISIL threat and fashion a decade-long effort that addresses the highly complex Iraq-Syria battlefield, as well as ISIL's global expansion.
- Develop a detailed political strategy for both countries, and use military support and other measures to advance it.
- Adopt a new approach to implementation that includes synchronizing authorities and greater effort to link the political and military lines of effort in Iraq and Syria.

CHAPTER TWO

The Counter-ISIL Strategy, the Political Context, and the Threat

The U.S. Counter-ISIL Strategy

The U.S. counter-ISIL strategy was first outlined in President Barack Obama's speech on September 10, 2014, and restated by Secretary Carter in congressional testimony on July 7, 2015.[1] The first line of effort outlines the fundamental political objectives necessary to achieve lasting defeat of ISIL: to build more effective, inclusive, and multisectarian governance in Iraq, and to reach a political solution to Syria's civil war. The second and third lines of effort describe the military effort, led by DoD, to deny ISIL safe havens and to build and enable partner forces in Iraq and Syria. The fourth line of effort is to enhance intelligence collection, and the fifth is to disrupt ISIL finances. Sixth and seventh are to counter ISIL messaging and disrupt the flow of foreign fighters. The eighth line of effort is to provide humanitarian support, and the ninth is to protect the U.S. homeland from ISIL attacks.

The Political Context

This analysis focuses on the military aspect of the counter-ISIL strategy and particularly the building and enabling of indigenous forces,

---

[1]   Ashton B. Carter, *Hearing to Receive Testimony on Counter-ISIL (Islamic State of Iraq and the Levant) Strategy*, transcript of the United States Committee on Armed Services before the United States Senate, Washington, D.C.: Alderson Reporting Company, July 7, 2015b.

which is deemed vital to achieving a lasting defeat of ISIL. The military aspects, however, are intertwined with the political aspects of the conflict, and the U.S. aspiration to encourage an inclusive Iraqi government as the essential "defeat" mechanism. The reasoning is that if Baghdad's central government becomes more inclusive by embracing Iraqi Sunnis, this will dampen the recruiting appeal of ISIL and encourage Sunnis to turn against the jihadists in their midst. Iraqi Prime Minister Haider al-Abadi articulated this aim in numerous speeches advocating a path of decentralization, foreseen in the Iraqi constitution, which has been called "functioning federalism."[2]

The barriers to achieving this vision of an inclusive Iraq, however, are high and will take time to overcome, if indeed Iraqis are able to embrace this path. The deep Sunni-Shia cleavages, the growing influence of Iran, and the chronic disunity among the Sunni tribes and political blocs all stand in the way of achieving this vision. An intra-Shia power struggle further complicates Prime Minister Abadi's governing prospects, although he has received solid support from the Grand Ayatollah Ali al-Sistani, who has curbed Shia militia groups' power, and thus implicitly Iran's attempts to manipulate Iraqi politics to its advantage.

It is possible that a solid core of the Shia parties that control the central government, including the parliament, will coalesce around Prime Minister Abadi's vision of decentralization and granting local autonomy to Sunni provinces. Parliament did approve a major revision of the provincial powers law (Law 21) in June 2013,[3] which directed sig-

---

2   Vice President Joe Biden used this term in his op-ed in the *Washington Post*, pledging U.S. support for it:

> Another approach that is emerging is a 'functioning federalism' under the Iraqi constitution, which would ensure equitable revenue-sharing for all provinces and establish locally rooted security structures, such as a national guard, to protect the population in cities and towns and deny space for ISIL while protecting Iraq's territorial integrity. (Joe Biden, "Iraqis Must Rise Above Their Differences to Rout Terrorists," *Washington Post*, August 22, 2014.)

3   See Reidar Visser, "Provincial Powers Law Revisions, Elections Results for Anbar and Nineveh: Is Iraq Headed for Complete Disintegration?" gulfanalysis.wordpress.com, June 27, 2013. Visser's post translates into English parts of Law 21, which was originally written

nificant devolution of seven ministries' authorities and responsibilities to the provinces. According to the law's vaguely worded Article 31-10,[4] security responsibilities are to be shared between the central and provincial government. Author conversations suggest that Sunni parties also may be moving to embrace a federal vision for Iraq, as opposed to harboring visions of reclaiming power in Baghdad, but mistrust runs deep on both sides. For the Sunnis' part, their list of grievances includes the brutal suppression of the Hawija protest in April 2013; the arrest and indictments of Sunni officials; the use of the de-Baathification law to bar Sunni political participation; and the failure to incorporate the "Sons of Iraq" into security forces or provide other gainful employment as agreed with the United States, which unilaterally armed Sunnis as local protectors during the 2007–2008 surge.[5] For the Shias' part, they harbor a well-grounded fear born of ISIL attacks launched from Sunni areas, Sunni revanchist movements, and long years of brutal suppression under Saddam Hussein's regime. Recent acts on both sides stoked fear and acts of vengeance, such as ISIL's 2014 slaughter of Shia recruits at the Speicher base near Tikrit, in which Sunni tribesmen from Al Ajeel were complicit.

On the security front, two vehicles provide a potential path for Sunnis' inclusion via incorporation into Iraqi security structures. The first was the formation of the *hashd al-shaabi*, or Popular Mobilization Forces (PMF). After ISIL swept through the west and took Mosul in June 2014, the Grand Ayatollah Ali al-Sistani, the senior Shia cleric of Iraq, called for Iraqis to fight against ISIL. His fatwa said that "citizens able . . . are to volunteer for the security forces to achieve this holy aim," but the effect was to spur a flood of Shia volunteers into the militia forces rather than the ISF. As analyst Kirk Sowell has noted, "Sistani was not giving Shia a mandate to wage war against Sunnis in

---

in Arabic. Visser is a research fellow at the Norwegian Institute of International Affairs and the editor of *Iraq and Gulf Analysis*.

[4]   Visser, 2013.

[5]   Linda Robinson, *Tell Me How This Ends: General David Petraeus and the Search for a Way Out of Iraq*, New York, N.Y.: PublicAffairs Books, 2008.

general, but rather to support the state."[6] The PMF are overwhelmingly Shia, but some 15,000 Sunni tribesmen have been enrolled in the PMF as of February 2016. The PMF is not a permanent vehicle for Sunni incorporation, however. No law has been passed to sanction its ad hoc creation, and Iraq's constitution prohibits militias. The Iraqi budget provides for salaries for the PMF, with funding allotted in proportion to the provincial population. Under this formula, some 30,000 Sunnis could be incorporated into the *hashd*.

Second, as a longer-term security mechanism, Prime Minister Abadi proposed the formation of a national guard that would provide each province with a local force commanded by provincial authorities. The fate of this proposal remains uncertain. The Council of Ministers approved the proposal, but the Council of Representatives' Shia majority subsequently revised the proposed law to place the national guard under the central control of the prime minister and the ministry of defense. That version carries dramatically less appeal for Sunni-majority provinces and potential Sunni recruits. This change reflected Iraq's Shia parties' ongoing fear that an armed entity under the command of Sunni provincial leadership could be used to attack Baghdad or Shia areas. When the Sunni speaker of parliament, Salim al-Jubouri, attempted to bring the bill to a vote in September, Shia militia groups who feared that the bill would also be a vehicle for their demobilization derailed it.

In Syria, the political struggle has largely revolved around Syrians' desire to remove Assad rather than fight ISIL. Theoretically, if Assad were removed and a transitional regime acceptable to most Syrians were installed, Syrians might then turn on ISIL. Assad's grip weakened significantly over 2015, but a surge in support from Iran and Russia late in the year appeared to ensure his control of the capital and the Latakia coastal region, and thus guarantee that at least a rump regime will survive. At least in the near term, Syria appears destined to be broken into subregional sectors controlled by different armed parties: the regime backed by Hezbollah, Russia, and Iran that aims to hold

---

[6] Kirk H. Sowell, "The Rise of Iraq's Militia State," CarnegieEndowment.org, April 23, 2015.

the coast, Homs, and Damascus; the Southern Front along Syria's Jordanian border; ANF in the north and center; ISIL in the east; and the Syrian Kurds in the northeastern border area.

The United States has hoped to achieve Assad's departure through negotiations based on the 2012 Geneva Communiqué to form a transitional government and hold elections. Diplomacy alone appeared unlikely to achieve that goal, particularly after the dramatically increased military backing that Russia began providing to the Syrian government in 2015. Increased military pressure appears necessary to alter Syrian regime calculations. These two guarantors of Assad may be willing to negotiate his departure, if the costs of maintaining him in power mount. Neither Russia nor Iran likely would relish the idea of putting more ground forces into the country to shore up the degraded Syrian forces, which have been bolstered by Iranian Quds Forces advisers, Lebanese Hezbollah forces, and Iraqi and Afghan militias. Terms of an eventual agreement would require recognition of Russian and Iranian interests. Russia likely would seek to retain a foothold and rights to the Tartus base, which gives it a presence in the eastern Mediterranean, and Iran likely would insist on the means to continue supporting Hezbollah in Lebanon. Agreement on a transitional government should include international guarantees for the protection of the Alawite population, which would ease their concerns about retaliation from Assad opponents. A peacekeeping force likely would be required to oversee any agreement.

One alternative to moving forward on a two-front war with explicit U.S. support would be to embrace Assad and Russia for the moment, to enlist their support against ISIL. Such a scheme would appear to have little chance of success and high risks of eroding an already weak U.S. position. As Assad himself is the central driver of the Syrian conflict, any common cause between the United States and the Assad regime would alienate the very ground forces the former has been trying to recruit, train, and equip for action against ISIL. The U.S. government would alienate not only the Syrians, but regional allies as well, to uncertain effect. Therefore, such an alliance would be a net negative.

The United States can also reap gains from the opprobrium heaped on Russia for its air war against moderate Syrian groups, which caused civilian casualties and thousands of additional migrants. Even after both parties agreed on a cessation of hostilities (excepting ISIL and ANF), Russian and Syrian airstrikes on moderate opposition areas continued. Additional developments dating from the summer of 2015 also created a new calculus for the battle in Syria, presaging greater allied commitment to addressing that theater of conflict. Turkey, the United Kingdom, and France entered the air war against ISIL in Syria. Turkey also expanded its permission for the United States to use its military bases for launching armed air strikes, rather than just surveillance flights. Aircraft flying from Turkey can reach the target areas in minutes, versus hours flying from the Persian Gulf. Turkey's entry into the air war against Syria was complicated by its simultaneous attacks on camps of the Kurdish Workers' Party (PKK), which is allied with the Syrian Kurds. The ending of the Turkish government's ceasefire with the PKK threatened to undermine efforts to create an Arab-Kurdish anti-ISIL front in Syria. Turkey pledged to support efforts to clear the remaining 98-kilometer stretch of the Syrian-Turkish border held by ISIL, but its motivations were likely aimed at halting the Syrian Kurds' westward advance from Tal Abyad.

Assessment of ISIL

ISIL has demonstrated significant resilience, tactical proficiency, and operational adaptability. Although its ability to administer the large territory and population under its control over the longer term remains to be seen, ISIL has thus far defied predictions that its atrocities or inability to govern would prompt a backlash or implosion. Even though as many as 20,000 fighters out of an estimated force of 20,000 to 32,000 were killed after U.S. airstrikes began in August 2014, ISIL has been able to regenerate and resupply its force through internal supply lines in

Syria and Iraq, and externally, primarily through Turkey.[7] U.S. officials estimated the number of ISIL fighters at 25,000 as of February 2016, which is less than the high-end figure of 32,000 but would indicate a net gain of 13,000 since the war began. As all these estimates are subject to debate, the primary point is that ISIL has managed to compensate for the attrition. If this trend continues, it also suggests that an attrition-based strategy will not succeed in defeating ISIL.

As the Figure 2.1 illustrates, Iraqi and Kurdish forces have wrested away 40 percent of the territory ISIL once held in Iraq and about 20 percent of its Syrian territory. Fighters regained territory in the largely Kurdish areas of northern Iraq and northern Syria, in the Arab cities of Tikrit and Baiji in central Iraq, and then in Ramadi, the capital of largely Sunni Anbar province in December 2015. ISIL remained deeply entrenched in two provincial capitals (Raqqa and Mosul), however, and was only ejected from the town of Baiji and Baiji Oil Refinery after a yearlong battle. ISIL also made important gains in western Syria in 2015, taking Palmyra and areas around Aleppo.

ISIL has a highly organized structure, including procedures for replacing leaders lost in battle.[8] Its fighters are tactically proficient, and the group has introduced new tactics and weapons, including the use of armored vehicle–borne improvised explosive devices (IEDs). ISIL is operationally adaptive, shifting between maneuver and guerrilla warfare as circumstances dictate and launching new or diversionary attacks to maintain momentum.

The Islamic State is a hybrid threat that has mastered unconventional tactics. Its highly developed media operations broadcast its battlefield exploits in gory detail. These play a major role in attracting some 1,000 recruits a month into Iraq and Syria and prompting pledges of allegiance from groups in Egypt, Libya, Nigeria, South Asia,

---

[7]   Director of National Intelligence James Clapper testified on February 26, 2015, to the U.S. Senate that U.S. intelligence estimated ISIL fighters at 20,000 to 32,000. (James Clapper, *Hearing to Receive Testimony on Worldwide Threats*, transcript of the U.S. Senate Armed Services Committee hearing, Washington, D.C.: Alderson Reporting Company, February 26, 2015).

[8]   Christoph Reuter, "The Terror Strategist: Secret Files Reveal the Structure of Islamic State," *Spiegel*, April 18, 2015.

Figure 2.1
Iraq and Syria: ISIL's Areas of Influence, August 2014 to February 2016

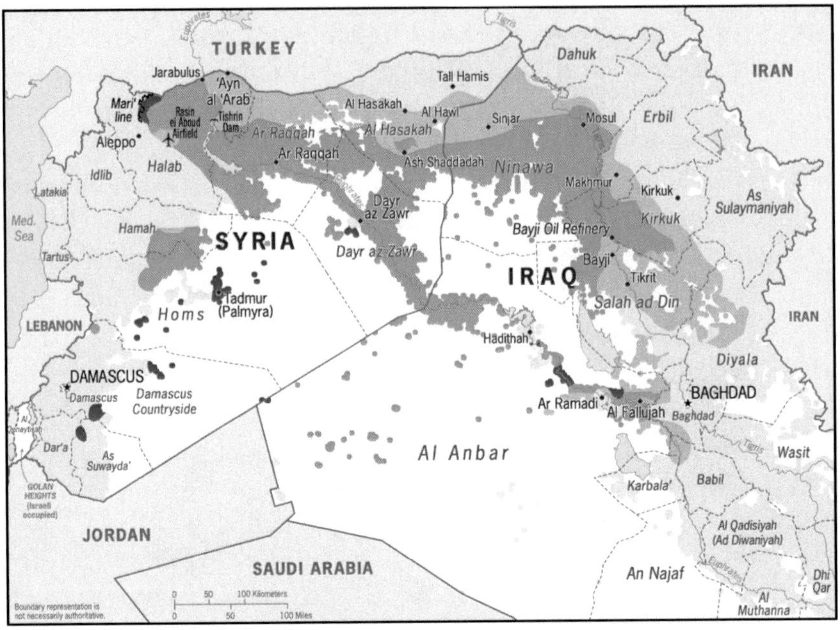

SOURCE: U.S. Department of Defense, "Operation Inherent Resolve: Targeted Operations Against ISIL Terrorists," March 15, 2016.
NOTES: Light orange = ISIL dominant; dark orange = ISIL territorial gain; green = ISIL territorial loss; gray = non-ISIL populated area; white = sparsely populated or unpopulated; dotted lines = administrative boundary.
RAND RR1290-2.1

and elsewhere. Of eight declared affiliates outside Iraq and Syria, the ISIL outpost in Libya is of greatest concern, having been supported by emissaries from core ISIL and reportedly manned by 5,000 to 6,000 fighters. Three attacks in Tunisia, France, and Kuwait on June 26, 2015, may have been inspired rather than directly orchestrated by ISIL, but they demonstrate the Islamic State's ability to stimulate action outside the main battlefield of Iraq and Syria. Nonetheless, the epicenter of the conflict is likely to remain those two countries, at least for the near future. This is because of the extensive territory, population, and resources that ISIL controls there; the heavily Iraqi character of the force, including a majority of its leadership; and the fact that ISIL has planted the flag of its declared caliphate in Raqqa, Syria.

ISIL is not without vulnerabilities. By holding territory, ISIL presents a target for conventional military power. Air strikes mounted by the United States and coalition forces have caused losses. ISIL staged a tactical retreat from Tikrit, the capital of Salah al-Din province in Iraq, after holding it for a year, and it has been pushed back from Kurdish areas in northern Iraq. The most notable reverse in the first half of 2015 has been the loss of territory along the Turkish-Syrian border to the Syrian Kurdish People's Defense Units (Kurdish *Yekineyen Parastina Gel* (YPG), which have joined with some Free Syrian Army (FSA) units in a loose alliance called Euphrates Volcano. Key ISIL leaders have been killed, including two top deputies and a financier in Syria known as Abu Sayyaf.[9] The chief effect of exploiting this vulnerability has been to push back ISIL toward guerrilla tactics, such as moving in smaller and disguised formations and using civilians to shield its major infrastructure from attack.

An even more important vulnerability for ISIL is the continued willingness of Sunnis to fight against it. Anti-ISIL forces held out in Ramadi for more than a year, until the government forces retreated in May, and provincial leaders have submitted lists of 22,000 Sunni volunteers willing to fight ISIL to the Iraqi government's Popular Mobilization Committee. The U.S.-led coalition thus far has been unable to effectively leverage this vulnerability to fight a population-centric war. Doing so would require the Iraqi government to reach out to Sunnis and undertake a more dispersed, unconventional approach to the war. Absent such an outreach, the most consequential internal contradiction that might cripple the organization would be an internecine war between the more Baathist elements with Iraqi-oriented objectives and the true believers set upon creating an apocalyptic caliphate.

Despite these facts, expectations that ISIL will inevitably self-destruct should be tempered. Many regimes have survived while inflicting unspeakable atrocities, governing poorly, and failing to feed

---

[9]   Karen DeYoung and Missy Ryan, "Senior ISIS Leader Killed in U.S. Raid in Syria," *Washington Post*, May 16, 2015.

subjects under their control. These circumstances, for example, could aptly describe the Saddam Hussein regime in Iraq. The degree of resilience that ISIL has demonstrated in the past year provides reasons to exercise caution regarding a prognosis of collapse. ISIL's staying power is relative in that the organization only needs to be stronger than its opponents, and when they are at odds, the bar is even lower. ISIL has proven able to regenerate leaders; resume resource production; obtain materiel through porous borders; and provide a modicum of food, services, and other goods. An autarkic economic model would permit it to subsist on internal resources, and one of the most potent weapons of recent conflicts has been homemade explosives. ISIL is thinking about sustainment in ambitious terms, as shown by its effort to create its own currency. While time and the current level of military pressure may increase the frictions within the organization, time also has allowed ISIL to entrench political and military systems and structures that allow it to control population and territory. Finally, the major source of resilience is the likelihood that, in the short term, sectarian tensions—fanned by numerous parties, including ISIL—will continue to motivate Sunnis to support and participate in or at least tolerate ISIL. With the estimated number of foreign fighters flocking to Iraq and Syria since 2012 topping 38,200, the hard fact is that ISIL has become an international movement.

CHAPTER THREE

Assessing the Counter-ISIL Forces

Counter-ISIL Forces in Iraq and Syria

The anti-ISIL forces on the ground in Iraq and Syria are characterized by limited capacity and capability, varying intentions, and an overall lack of coordination among them. This section describes and assesses the various anti-ISIL forces' capabilities and motivations, which are summarized in Table 3.1 at the end of this chapter. The principal forces in Iraq are: the army, the CTS, the Kurdish forces, and the PMF, comprising primarily Shia militias but also a nascent Sunni tribal force. Iraq's army suffers from numerous critical and structural weaknesses to include insufficient troops, poor leadership, a high incidence of corruption and low morale. Remedying these deficits will take time. The other government forces (police, CTS, Kurdish *Peshmerga*) can play supporting roles, but they cannot serve as the main force. Because of mistrust and resentment, neither the Iraq nor the Kurdish government has provided more than minimal support to Sunni tribes that wish to fight ISIL.

One of the largest entities currently fighting ISIL is the PMF, which includes long-standing Shia militia groups, the leaders of which are acting as battlefield commanders of the PMF. Media reports have documented their significant roles in Diyala, Jurf al-Sakhar, Salah al-Din, and Anbar, including at times the presence of Iranian Quds Force commander Qassem Soleimani. The PMF and the militia commanders have reaped significant political benefit as saviors of the country in a time of national emergency. The role of the Shia militias is problematic, however, as they have a record of committing abuses against

Sunnis, and their mere presence is viewed as an Iranian incursion. Despite their trepidation, some Sunni leaders have called for cooperation with Shia militias, including in Anbar, as they have lost faith in the ability of the ISF to do the job.[1] While the Shia militias played an important role in the first year of the counter-ISIL fight, a variety of Iraqi political leaders—from the Sunni president of the Council of Representatives to the Shia cleric and political leader Muqtada al-Sadr—have called for their integration into the regular forces or their demobilization to avoid permanent militia dominance of the security and political landscapes.

In Syria, anti-ISIL forces are plagued by even greater weaknesses in capacity and capability, mixed intentions, and lack of coordination. Most Syrians, as noted above, are primarily interested in fighting the Assad regime. The Syria Train and Equip program established criteria requiring trainees to pledge to fight ISIL, not Assad forces. Most forces are increasingly coalescing around Islamist anti-Assad fronts backed by Saudi Arabia, Qatar, and Turkey. Those who do want to fight ISIL are extremely fragmented and uncoordinated, although some efforts have been made to create umbrella groups and alliances that effectively aggregate combat power. Their current weakness renders them vulnerable, however, to both regime forces and Islamist extremist organizations that either target them or siphon off fighters.

Iraq's Anti-ISIL Forces

The Iraqi Security Forces

The ISF is beset by numerous capacity, capability, and structural weaknesses, including understrength units, inadequate recruiting, poor leadership and morale, lack of accountability, and equipment shortages. According to documents from the U.S. Embassy's Office of Security Cooperation, Iraq has, on paper, an army of 14 divisions—one armored, three mechanized, and ten infantry. Four divisions disintegrated with the rout in Mosul in June 2014, but the numbers of sol-

---

[1]   Mustafa Habib, "Tough Choices: Everyone Agrees, Shiite Militias Must Be Invited to Fight in Ramadi," Niquash.org, May 21, 2015.

diers present for duty had been dwindling before that event.[2] Iraq's ten divisions are undermanned, and exact statistics on the numbers actually present for duty are elusive. Estimates of actual serving soldiers range from 54,000 to 81,000. Thousands of other unfilled positions are called *ghost soldiers*, for whom salaries are paid. The funds either go into officers' pockets or are used to pay for legitimate but unfunded needs. Some poor officers have been fired, and while there are good officers, many substandard officers remain on the job, and some serve in critical positions. The Iraqi army is also top-heavy, with an estimated 1,300 brigadier generals (compared with 300 in the U.S. Army). The Iraqi army essentially stopped training in 2010, commanders were selected based on political rather than professional criteria, and many of the Iraqi soldiers the United States had trained were no longer in the force. These factors all degraded the force substantially by 2014.

Ministry of Interior police forces do not have a combat mission and will not play a primary role in clearing operations, but they would be an important element for hold operations and some counterterrorist actions. Information on the Federal Police's current size and equipment status is scarce, but one report estimated their strength at 36,000.[3] The Ministry of Interior has requested equipment from the United States, which had prioritized the resupply of the Iraqi military. While the U.S. forces do not currently train or advise any Federal Police units, Italy has begun to provide advisory support with personnel from its *carabinieri* (Italian national police). Shia political parties and militias have historically strongly influenced both the staffing and the policies of the Ministry of Interior, and a Badr representative is currently the minister.

U.S. advisers have not been able to fully inventory the equipment, weapons, and ammunition the ISF possess, but based on the amounts that U.S. and coalition partners have supplied, Iraq currently has ample stocks of ammunition and small arms. Heavy weapons and

---

[2] Michael Knights, "The Future of Iraq's Armed Forces," Baghdad, Iraq: Al-Bayan Center for Planning and Studies, March 2016. In addition, an assessment conducted by the U.S. military concluded that 26 of 50 brigades could be "reputable partners" once reequipped and trained.

[3] International Institute of Strategic Studies, *The Military Balance 2016*, London: Routledge, 2016.

armored vehicles are scarce. Prime Minister Abadi stated that 2,300 high-mobility multipurpose wheeled vehicles (HMMWVs) were seized by ISIL after troops fled Mosul in June 2014, and some of those have been employed in Ramadi and elsewhere as powerful bombs.[4] Iraq's air capacity and capability are also limited. The Iraqi air force has Cessna Caravans, 12 Su-25 jets, and eight C-130s. A major U.S. sale of 36 F-16s to Iraq resulted in the delivery of the first four in July 2015, but only four pilots completed training. One of the pilots died in an F-16 crash in Arizona just as they completed training. Rotary-wing aviation is primarily Russian Mi-28 and Mi-17 and Bell helicopters.

The disposition of the ISF has been primarily defensive. More than 40 percent of the ISF is assigned to the Baghdad Operations Command, reflecting both the government's priority of defending the capital and its assessment that ISIL can indeed threaten it. A third rationale is a political calculation to balance the Ministry of Interior forces in Baghdad. Finally, the Baghdad Operations Command recently has been assigned responsibility for retaking parts of eastern Anbar from ISIL. Another significant portion of the ISF is deployed in Diyala and the Shia provinces to the south.

Counter-Terrorism Service

The CTS, Iraq's special operations element, has been the main Iraqi government force conducting offensive operations since the counter-ISIL campaign began. The CTS has long been considered the most capable element of the Iraqi forces, although it was misused for partisan and sectarian purposes under the previous government. Despite this misuse, the CTS maintained the mixed composition of Sunni, Shia, and Kurdish fighters that has characterized it since its formation. In the past two years, the CTS has performed with distinction, if not heroically; because of the weakness of the Iraqi army and police forces, it has shouldered a disproportionate share of the anti-ISIL campaign. Since December 2013, the CTS has been deployed in every major battle. As of May 2015, according to CTS records, the CTS had

---

[4]   Alexander Smith, "Iraqi PM Haider Al-Abadi Says Forces Lost 2,300 Humvees to ISIS," NBCNews.com, June 1, 2015.

incurred 2,636 casualties, which reduced its fighting force to somewhere between 6,000 and 7,000 troops from its authorized level of 11,000.[5]

CTS forces are overemployed and inadequately supported by other forces. In many instances they have been employed incorrectly, in small numbers in fixed positions, rather than in the commando operations for which they were designed. They are performing infantry tasks in the absence of sufficient trained, capable army troops. For example, CTS forces were pinned down in Baiji's oil refinery for months without relief and watched more than two dozen of their wounded comrades die. This experience probably influenced their decision to withdraw from Ramadi under the ISIL assault in May.

The CTS is under great stress as a result of this constant employment and inadequate support from other units. A number of U.S. Special Operations Forces (SOF) advisers believe that the CTS could crumble under the strain, if the way in which its forces are employed and supported does not change.[6] To rebuild the force, the U.S. and coalition SOF advisers have revised the training program to add more classes of shorter duration. The CTS headquarters projects that by January 2016, the ranks of the three Iraqi special operations brigades will be back to 11,000 on duty and 2,000 in the selection and training pipeline, net of attrition. The compressed training means the newer force will be trained as light infantry and will be less experienced. While the CTS does have two forward observers and is training 14 more, the initial proficiency of the new controllers will be limited.

There are frictions between the CTS and the Ministry of Defense, partly because these are separate organizations. Parliament has not provided the CTS its own separate budget, so its funding has been precarious. The CTS's current urgent needs are armored HMMWVs—it is short by 1,400, according to its formal equipping table, but can repair a number of those damaged and recovered, if it can acquire the spare parts. The unit also lacks machine guns (.50 caliber, M240s, M249s)

---

[5]   Statistics provided by U.S. Embassy Office of Security Cooperation–Iraq and corroborated with CTS commander general Taleb Kenani.

[6]   Special operations advisers, interviews with the author, five locations in Iraq, May 2015.

and the spare parts to repair damaged ones. The Iraq Train and Equip Fund package includes HMMWVs, but they were not readily available because of limited U.S. production capacity. Machine guns were available in U.S. Army stocks in Kuwait, but as with the HMMWVs, the United States and Iraq will have to decide whether to prioritize delivery to CTS or ISF brigades.

Kurdish Security Forces

The Kurdish Security Forces (KSF) include the *Peshmerga* and the interior ministry Zerevani. They are valiant, motivated, and capable forces that have pushed back ISIL in northern Iraq, and in the process, expanded territory held by the Kurdistan Regional Government by 30 percent. They also supported Syrian Kurds fighting in Syrian territory. They have, however, largely achieved their objectives of defending predominantly Kurdish areas and have moved into defensive mode. ISIL will certainly continue to test their defensive line, which stretches 1,200 kilometers. But the KSF are likely to play only a supporting role in any offensive to liberate Mosul, and they have not yet committed explicitly to a number of specific requests for supporting roles in that operation. Moreover, they are not likely to deploy to Anbar or other purely Arab areas. Therefore, it should not be seen as a force that can substitute or compensate for the shortcomings of the Arab forces.

U.S. forces are supporting the KSF through a combined operations center and advisory support at multiple echelons. This includes advisory support to the brigade level.[7] The Kurds seek heavy weaponry, and the United States will have to decide how to prioritize the many requests it has received. Some U.S. officials think that the Kurds are relatively well supplied at this time, especially compared with other elements seeking support. According to U.S. records, the KSF has

---

[7] Most of the KSF are not organized along conventional military organizational lines; they tend to fight in company or smaller-sized units. The units may be formed provisionally, and fighters will often leave the front lines to work a job for a period to support their families, and then return to the front. A typical pattern is one week's duty followed by two weeks' leave. Thus their present-for-duty numbers are lower than advertised. SOF are advising the sector commanders, which roughly equate to brigade commanders, and are able to assist with fire support from forward command posts on relatively fixed front lines.

received at least 50 million rounds of ammunition, thousands of small arms, and more than 8,500 antitank weapons donated by coalition countries directly to the KSF.

Sunni Tribal Forces

The program to raise Sunni tribal forces to fight ISIL proceeded slowly in 2015, although efforts were made to energize it following the fall of Ramadi in May 2015. As of July 2015, some 22,000 Sunnis had been nominated by their provinces to serve, but only half that number had been approved, about 5,400 officially enrolled and paid, and only 3,000 had been armed. An even smaller number (about 2,300) was receiving advisory assistance from U.S. forces at the time, as the tribesmen must first pass two U.S. vetting processes.[8] The pace of arming Sunnis increased, however, following the fall of Ramadi, with an initial 800 armed at Al-Taqaddum Air Base in Anbar in May, followed by classes of 500 every two weeks. By March 2016, 15,000 Sunni tribesmen had been enlisted, 10,000 of them in Anbar province.

Even if all Sunni volunteers are incorporated into the PMF, they will not be heavily armed, equipped with armored vehicles, or trained for combined arms maneuvers. They will primarily serve as local defense forces, though they can have greater military effect if coordinated with other forces.

The only place where such synergy between the ISF and Sunni tribes has been achieved to date is in western Anbar, where the Iraqi Seventh Army, the al-Jazeera and al-Badia Command, and elements of four tribes mentored by coalition SOF are working together. By contrast, neither the Mosul Fighting Forces (MFF), another group recruited from former policemen, nor Sunni tribes recruited in the north were receiving salaries, arms, ammunition, or other support from either the Iraqi or the Kurdish governments as of May 2015. The MFF was subsequently dissolved.

The arming of Sunnis would provide a strong signal about the Iraqi government's commitment to inclusivity, and their intelligence

---

[8]   One vetting process ascertains that no member is credibly alleged to have committed human rights abuses as required by the Leahy Amendment, and the other ascertains that the inductee has no ties to Iran, al Qaeda, or its successors in Iraq.

value would be substantial. Even small numbers of Sunni forces could be employed in unconventional ways that might achieve significant effect. In the government budget adopted in December 2015, Iraq committed that 30 percent of the PMF would be raised from the provinces where the ISIL fight is occurring, which translates to a commitment to include some 30,000 Sunnis. The Sunnis' inclusion in the PMF would be helpful, so long as long-term programs are also fashioned to incorporate Sunnis into the regular forces. The Sons of Iraq program of 2006–2010 failed to do so because the Iraqi government did not embrace the agreed-upon transition mechanisms and, above all, the idea that Iraq would be more secure with more Sunnis serving in the duly-constituted security forces.[9] One idea from the surge period that might be revisited is the commitment to deploy Sunnis recruited into the Iraqi Army in their home provinces, at least for initial tours.[10] That would avoid the build-up of provisional forces that would later need to be incorporated into permanent security forces, whether army, police, or some type of national guard.

Shia Militias and Popular Mobilization Forces

The Iraqi Shia armed groups are motivated, organized, and well equipped. They number some 80,000–100,000[11] and comprise three elements: (1) the volunteers who responded to Ayatollah Sistani's call to defend the country, (2) a collection of newer Shia militias, and (3) the long-standing Shia groups—the Badr Organization, the Kata'ib Hizballah (KH), the Asa'ib Ahl al-Haq (AAH), and the Sadrist Peace Brigade.[12]

---

[9] Robinson, 2008, pp. 320–353.

[10] Robinson, 2008, pp. 273, 352–353.

[11] For one source using the 100,000-troop estimate, see Kenneth Katzman and Carla E. Humud, "Iraq: Politics and Governance," Congressional Research Service, September 16, 2015.

[12] The Badr and Sadr elements are established political parties with paramilitary forces. The Badr Corps formed in 1982 with Iranian support to fight Saddam Hussein in the Iran-Iraq war. In 2011, Badr split from the Islamic Supreme Revolutionary Council of Iraq in order to become a separate politico-military organization. Members of the Badr Corps were included in the first Iraqi units formed after the U.S. invasion, the Iraqi Civil Defense Corps, which

After leading Shia cleric Grand Ayatollah Ali al-Sistani issued a call for Iraqis to defend their country last summer, many of these militias were reinvigorated, and Shia volunteers in particular responded to Sistani's call. The Iraqi government formed a Popular Mobilization Committee to organize these PMF. This has been the nominal vehicle for corralling the disparate paramilitary forces, both Shia and Sunni. Prime Minister Abadi is formally the commander in chief of the PMF, and the chain of command goes from him to his national security adviser to the KH commander, then to whatever field chain they designate. The United States requests that any PMF that wish to receive air support must fall under the Iraqi military chain of command in order to receive such support. After the fall of Ramadi, the council of ministers approved a plan that included a requirement that Iraqi military forces exercise command and control over all the battlefield forces.

Badr, KH, and AAH have been at the forefront of PMF activity in Diyala, Salah al-Din, Baghdad, and Anbar provinces. Furthermore, al-Muhandis is the deputy chief of the government's overall coordinating body, the Popular Mobilization Committee. He and Badr leader (and member of parliament) Hadi al-Amiri have visited the Baghdad command center. They and Khazali regularly appear on the battlefield. A representative from the Popular Mobilization Committee reportedly sits in the Baghdad Combined Joint Operations Center.

The Iranian links to these Shia militia groups, and their implication in deaths of U.S. troops in earlier years, poses a significant issue for the United States. In addition, the behavior of the Shia militias in

---

later became the Iraqi Army. During the U.S. invasion in 2003, Moqtada al-Sadr founded another politico-military organization, whose militias were largely demobilized after 2010 or converted into social service organizations until the upsurge of ISIL violence in 2014. Badr is part of the dominant State of Law coalition, while the Sadrists won 32 seats in the April 2014 elections. Kataib Hizbollah was trained by Iran's Quds Force, as was Asaib Ahl al-Haq, a splinter group of the Sadr's original militia, the Mahdi Army. KH commander Abu Mahdi al-Muhandis is on the U.S. Treasury's list of specially designated terrorists, and Qais Khazali was detained by U.S. forces for the death of five U.S. troops in 2007. According to chair of the Joint Chiefs of Staff GEN Martin Dempsey's July 7, 2015, testimony, during the 2003–2010 war, Iranian-backed groups also were allegedly involved in the deaths of approximately 500 U.S. troops. (See Carter, 2015c.) A short history of these groups can be found in Katzman and Humud (2015).

committing abuses against Sunnis is highly problematic. The newer Shia militias are, according to some, less anti-American, but many are splinters from the main Iranian-backed groups. The United States has decided to provide air support to those units that submit to the Iraqi government chain of command, but more active coordination with those units could produce greater effects in countering ISIL. The PMF has become popular and increasingly powerful, so the challenge is exploit their battlefield utility in the short term while simultaneously encouraging plans for their demobilization or integration into regular professional forces. The risks of the Lebanonization of Iraq should give pause to Iraqis across the spectrum.

Syrian Opposition Forces

The New Syrian Forces (NSF) were those elements recruited, trained, and equipped by U.S. SOF under the ITEF legislation, which envisioned producing 15,000 fighters over three years. The lengthy recruitment and vetting process meant that the first forces were not trained until the summer of 2015. Some of the trainees left the training sites outside of Syria, with the result that only 60 recruits were trained and equipped by June 2015. The first 54 were inserted into northern Syria, near Aleppo, on July 17.[13] Another pool of 7,000 recruits would produce additional trainees for the remainder of the year. The central hurdle for this program, however, was its viability given the constraints imposed: Most Syrians are interested in fighting the Assad regime rather than ISIL, yet the vetting criteria requires that trainees agree to direct their efforts against Islamic State. After a series of mishaps, including an attack on the fielded forces by the ANF, and NSF's ceding of equipment to the ANF, the program was suspended, with some officials suggesting that it might be revived to train small numbers in forward air control to assist existing groups.[14]

---

[13] Ahmed Shiwesh, "U.S.-Trained Rebels Rejoin the Fight North Syria," Aranews.com, July 18, 2015.

[14] Michael Shear, Helene Cooper, and Eric Schmitt, "Obama Administration Ends Effort to Train Syrians to Combat ISIS," *New York Times,* October 9, 2015.

People's Defense Units/Syrian Democratic Forces

As mentioned above, the YPG and some FSA units recently allied in a collaboration called *Burkan al-Furat* (Euphrates Volcano) and subsequently the Syrian Democratic Forces (SDF). In the spring and summer of 2015, the allied groups made significant gains on the Turkish border, notably the capture of Tal Abyad, which severed ISIL's main external line of communication. The YPG's Kurdish composition may limit its reach or prompt a political backlash in Arab areas. The Turkish government opposes the YPG and its parent party, the Democratic Union Party, which is linked to the Turkish Kurdistan Workers' Party. The YPG is a well-organized force that claims to have more than 35,000 fighters; it receives air and ISR support from the U.S.-led coalition.[15] In October 2015, following the suspension of the NSF training program, the United States decided to support the SDF with weapons and, for the first time, air-dropped 50 tons of materiel into northern Syria to facilitate their campaign to press south toward Raqqa. As of March 2016, approximately 7,000 Syrian Arab fighters had joined the SDF. However, it is unclear whether the SDF, so long as it remains predominantly Kurdish, will be able to take and hold Raqqa or other Arab areas, and whether Turkey would tolerate such advances, particularly on its border.

Free Syrian Army

The FSA comprises eight to ten major groups and hundreds of small factions that once represented the majority of the moderate opposition forces (it absorbed the Free Officers Movement after 2011). Their ranks, once estimated at 45,000–80,000, have been substantially thinned by attrition and defections to other groups. No reliable estimates exist of the FSA's current strength, but it may have dwindled to fewer than 20,000. The FSA was always a loose umbrella of groups following individual leaders in regional fronts, and that fragmentation was exacerbated by competition between Saudi Arabia and Qatar, the principal external backers. The United States also supplied nonlethal aid, and

---

[15] Aaron Lund, "Syria's Kurdish Army: An Interview with Redur Khalil," CarnegieEndowment.org, December 25, 2013.

tube-launched, optically tracked, wireless-guided (TOW) missiles, to the FSA. Infighting, poor leadership, and loss of control of arms and nonlethal supplies have all plagued the FSA, which bore the brunt of the Assad regime's attacks. One enduring element of the FSA formation, however, the Southern Front, gained significant territory in the populated southwestern part of Syria until the Russian intervention began to erode its control. The Southern Front has received U.S. and Jordanian support and comprises 58 smaller groups, a reflection of the highly localized nature of the Syrian opposition. The FSA has allied with the Christian Syriac Military Council, and some FSA elements in northern Syria also cooperate with YPG. While the Southern Front remained the strongest element of the FSA, Russia's military intervention sliced deeply into its stronghold on the Jordanian border.

Al-Nusra Front/Army of Conquest

The Islamist ANF is the principal rival to ISIL in Syria, following the group's split in 2013. The ANF, estimated at 10,000 fighters, gained significant momentum in 2014–2015 by attracting outside funding and affiliates, including Ahrar al-Sham and seven others in an alliance called the *Jaish al-Fatah* (Army of Conquest). Their combined fighting force might reach 20,000 to 25,000.

ISIL and the ANF, which is an al Qaeda affiliate, hold the most territory. The regime forces and the secular opposition FSA/Southern Front, however, hold significant populated areas in western Syria. Most Syrian fighters under banners other than ISIL's have as their primary objective the removal of Syrian President Bashar al-Assad. At this time, Assad's departure likely would favor ANF and ISIL. The armed opposition in Syria is extremely fragmented, but over the past year, the ANF's gains may be positioning it as the principal anti-Assad opposition force. The same groups that joined with ANF might be peeled off, provided that a new alliance could demonstrate momentum and backing. ISIL holds less-populated territory in eastern Syria, though it has made inroads in the northwest over the past year.

Table 3.1
Characteristics of Counter-ISIL Forces

Name	Estimated Size and Composition	Equipment	Capability/Missions Relative Capability Level (High/Medium/Low)	Political Disposition and Support Shared U.S. Interests (High/Medium/Low)
Iraqi Security Forces (ISF) (Iraq)	64,000–100,000, including 54,000–80,000 Iraqi Army 14 divisions (one armored, three mechanized, ten infantry) and Ministry of Interior Police Forces with 36,000	Ample stocks of ammunition and small arms. Heavy weapons and armored vehicles are scarce. Iraqi Air Force has 12 Su-25 jets, ten ISR platforms, 15 C-130s and six An32-B medium. Four F-16s were delivered in July 2015 and began operations in September. Rotary wing includes 29 Russian Mi-28, Mi-35 attack and Mi-17 and Bell helicopters	Likely able to hold Baghdad, but alone is unlikely able to retake Anbar or Ninewa. Mission is primarily defensive, more than 40 percent are assigned to the Baghdad Operations Center, a reflection of the government's priority of defending the capital Capability: Low/medium	Many units are still under strength after disintegration in summer 2014. Many officers were selected based on political rather than professional criteria. Many of the soldiers trained (before 2011) by the United States are no longer in the force. Brigades recently trained by coalition forces reportedly performed well in Anbar operations Shared interests: High

Table 3.1—Continued

Name	Estimated Size and Composition	Equipment	Capability/Missions Relative Capability Level (High/Medium/Low)	Political Disposition and Support Shared U.S. Interests (High/Medium/Low)
Counter-Terrorism Service (CTS) (Iraq)	8,000; comprising Sunni, Shia, and Kurdish fighters	Currently some 8,000 strong, CTS is rebuilding to its authorized level of 11,000. Battlefield casualties reduced available forces to approximately 6,000 in 2015. CTS also suffers shortages of armored vehicles and medium and heavy machine guns (.50 caliber, M240s, M249s) and spare parts	Shouldering disproportionate share of anti-ISIL campaign because of weakness in Iraqi Army and police forces. Overemployed and inadequately supported by other forces Capability: High	Tensions exist between CTS and Ministry of Defense because they are separate organizations. U.S. and coalition SOF advisers have revised training, adding more classes of shorter duration in an attempt to rebuild the force Shared interests: High

Name	Estimated Size and Composition	Equipment	Capability/Missions Relative Capability Level (High/Medium/Low)	Political Disposition and Support Shared U.S. Interests (High/Medium/Low)
Kurdish Security Forces (KSF), *Peshmerga* (Iraq)	113,000 fighters (not all on duty simultaneously)	Heavy weaponry stocks include tanks, howitzers, and rocket artillery; some unarmored light helicopters. The United States has supplied small arms, light antitank weapons, and ammunition. Germany is supplying helmets and body armor, assault rifles, trucks, armored vehicles, light antitank weapons, guided antiarmor launchers, and missiles. UK/France supplied automatic cannons/heavy machine guns. Iran has supplied weapons and ammunition	Kurdish forces pushed back ISIL in northern Iraq, in the process expanding territory held by the Kurdistan Regional Government by 30 percent. Also supported Syrian Kurds fighting in Syrian territory. They have largely achieved their objectives of defending predominantly Kurdish areas, though they have pledged to play a supporting role in retaking Mosul Capability: High	U.S. forces are supporting KSF through a combined operations center and advisory support at multiple echelons, including advisory support to the brigade level. Several countries are supporting KSF, and some U.S. offices think that they are relatively well supplied compared with other elements seeking support Shared interests: High

Name	Estimated Size and Composition	Equipment	Capability/Missions Relative Capability Level (High/Medium/Low)	Political Disposition and Support Shared U.S. Interests (High/Medium/Low)
Sunni Tribal Forces (Iraq)	15,000 forces enrolled as of March 2016. Not all have been supplied with arms by Iraqi government	Not heavily armed, equipped with armored vehicles, or trained for combined arms maneuvers	Program run by Iraqi government as part of the PMF. Will primarily serve as local defense forces, though they can have greater effect if coordinated with other forces, such as in western Anbar

Capability: Low | Early efforts to organize Sunnis in the north lacked salaries, arms, and support from the Iraqi and Kurdish governments. The arming of Sunnis would provide a strong signal of the Iraqi government's commitment to inclusivity

Shared interests: High |
| Popular Mobilization Forces (Iraq) | 100,000; includes new groups and previously formed Shia militias, such as the Badr Organization, KH, and AAH | Primarily Shia volunteers and militias. Motivated, organized, and well equipped. Small arms, armored vehicles, IEDs, rocket-propelled grenades (RPGs), improvised rocket-assisted mortars, rockets, M1A1 Abrams tanks, armored HMMWVs, and M113 armored personnel vehicles | Active in Diyala, Salah al-Din, Baghdad, and Anbar provinces. Defense units in south and protecting Shia shrines. Iran has supplied equipment and advisers to militias. Badr and KH have some 20,000 fighters each

Capability: Medium | The Iraqi government formed a Popular Mobilization Committee (PMC) to oversee the PMF. Iranian links to some of the Shia militias, and their implication in the deaths of U.S. troops in earlier years, poses a significant issue for the United States. The current request by the United States is that the reporting chain for these groups goes to the ISF chain of command, if they wish to receive air support in ISF-led operations

Shared interests: Low |

Name	Estimated Size and Composition	Equipment	Capability/Missions Relative Capability Level (High/Medium/Low)	Political Disposition and Support Shared U.S. Interests (High/Medium/Low)
People's Defense Unit (Syrian Kurdish Yekineyen Parastina Gel or YPG)/ Syrian Democratic Forces (SDF) (Syria)	40,000 fighters (33,000–35,000 YPG and 7,000 Syrian Arab Coalition allied in SDF umbrella	Primarily small arms, artillery, and some armored vehicles	Made significant gains on the Turkish border, notably the capture of Tal Abyad, and with it, the closure of ISIL's main external line of communication. Capture of towns around Raqqa including Shaddadi, Al Hawl. Fighting over remaining 90 km of Turkish-Syrian border controlled by ISIL Capability: Medium	Receives air and ISR support from the U.S.-led coalition. Kurdish composition may limit its reach or prompt a political backlash in Arab areas. The Turkish government opposes the YPG, which is linked to the Turkish Kurdistan Workers' Party Shared interests: High
Free Syrian Army (FSA) (Syria)	Current size unknown. Umbrella group once estimated at 45,000–60,000, but thinned by attrition and defections to other groups	Antitank missiles provided by the West were reportedly captured by ANF; primarily small arms, mortars, artillery, and captured Syrian army tanks and armored personnel carriers	Primarily fights Assad regime. Formed originally from Syrian army defectors, the FSA has some 2,500 factions. The Southern Front has been most cohesive. Some northern elements have supplied fighters to the SDF. Has sustained the brunt of the Assad regime's attacks Capability: Medium	The United States began providing overt nonlethal assistance in 2013. The Southern Front has received U.S. and Jordanian support Shared interests: High
al-Nusra Front (ANF) (Syria)	10,000, possibly 20,000 with allies	Captured antitank missiles, tanks, armored personnel carriers, artillery, mortars, and small arms	al Qaeda affiliate and the principal rival to ISIL in Syria. It has engaged in sporadic fighting with ISIL Capability: High	ANF gains and its attraction of new allies under may be positioning it as the principal anti-Assad opposition force Shared interests: Low

CHAPTER FOUR

Assessment of the Counter-ISIL Campaign

Between August 2014 and March 2016, Iraqi and Syrian ground forces, backed by coalition airpower, drove ISIL out of 40 percent of the territory it had seized in Iraq and 10 percent of the territory it held in Syria. Much of this territory was open, rural terrain in northern Syria and Iraq. Key crossroads for ISIL in Syria were retaken: Kobani, Tal Abyad, Al-Hawl, and Shaddadi. And in Iraq, the cities of Tikrit, Baiji, Sinjar, and Ramadi were retaken. Some 90 senior and mid-level ISIL leaders, such as provincial *walis* and *emirs*, and key facilitators, such as the oil-and-gas emir known as Abu Sayyaf, were killed. A senior deputy to ISIL leader Abu Bakr al-Baghdadi known as Hajji Mutazz was the most-senior figure killed in an airstrike. "Jihadi John," a notorious figure who beheaded hostages in videos, and Junaid Hussain, who had orchestrated external attack plans and the leaking of U.S. servicemen's personal data, also were killed. For the most part, for the first 16 months of the campaign, ISIL leaders adapted quickly to hide in the urban terrain where U.S. airstrikes could not reach them without causing massive civilian casualties.

These gains notwithstanding, the cities of Raqqa, Mosul, and Fallujah remained firmly in ISIL's grip, and ISIL seized Palmyra and other locations in the populated areas of western Syria. The group was also accused of bombings in Turkey, attacks in Belgium and Paris, and some level of association with other attacks in Tunisia, Egypt, Libya, and elsewhere. The recruitment of new fighters continued to replace the losses suffered on the battlefield, and sufficient logistical support enabled ISIL to maintain its operations and control of the remaining territory. The massive intelligence trove seized with the raid on Abu Sayyaf, in which he was killed, enabled the coalition in the fall of 2015 to mount Operation Tidal Wave, an air campaign targeting oil and gas separation plants, hundreds of fuel trucks, and other key resource nodes. The U.S. government estimated that about half of ISIL's $1 billion annual revenues come from oil and gas, and that the wave of attacks had significantly reduced this source of income. However, earlier attempts to stem the oil production led ISIL to proliferate a number of "mom-and-pop" refining locations and rebuild its infrastructure, so the long-term effects remain to be seen.

The Abu Sayyaf raid and Operation Tidal Wave marked an important inflection point in the campaign, characterized by a shift toward a more intelligence-driven approach to air power. Up to that point, the vast majority of airstrikes had been employed in support of ground forces and often struck targets of primarily tactical value. From August 2014 to mid-March 2016, 10,962 airstrikes had been conducted: 7,336 in Iraq and 3,626 in Syria.[1] The great majority of the strikes in Syria were launched in the battle for Kobani from October 2015 to January 2016. This approach to the use of airpower was dictated to a certain degree by the lack of intelligence to pinpoint more strategic targets as well as the need to support troops in contact. Advisers reported that indigenous forces often waited to move until air cover was available and/or forces firing upon them were struck.

A further acceleration of the military campaign occurred after Defense Secretary Ash Carter announced in congressional testimony on December 1, 2015, that some 100 special operators would be sent to Iraq as part of an expeditionary targeting force that would conduct raids alongside Iraqi partner forces with the permission of the Iraqi government.[2] In Iraq, they would be allowed to conduct unilateral

---

[1]   U.S. Central Command statistics updated periodically. See U.S. Department of Defense, 2016. As of March 17, 2016, a total of 22,779 were reported as damaged or destroyed (139 tanks, 374 HMMWVs, 1,162 staging areas, 5,894 buildings, 7,118 fighting positions, 1,272 oil infrastructure, and 6,820 targets characterized as "other.")

[2]   U.S. House of Representatives, Committee on Armed Services, "Hearing on U.S. Strategy for Syria and Iraq and its Implications for the Region," Washington, D.C., December 1, 2015b.

operations.[3] This stepped-up involvement produced further notable captures and deaths of ISIL leaders in the spring of 2016, including a top deputy, Haji Iman (or Abd al-Rahman Muhammad Mustafa al-Qaduli), and the military commander Omar al-Shishani. The accelerating campaign against the ISIL leadership raised the prospect that this important line of effort might outrun the advances in building a competent and coherent hold force in both Iraq and Syria, as well as the necessary political agreements to assure that new terrorist and insurgent activity would not emerge to fill the vacuum left by ISIL's demise.

The slow pace of progress over the campaign's first 18 months can be attributed to several factors. Three features stand out when surveying the course of the counter-ISIL campaign. First, the "Iraq first, Syria second" sequencing did not lend itself to seeking synergies between the two fronts. ISIL erased the border between Iraq and Syria and freely resupplied fighters and materiel in both directions. While a single commander was appointed for both countries, the decision was made to prioritize operations in Iraq.[4] The prioritization was premised on the idea that a more-capable ground force existed in Iraq, and headway could be made more easily there. This proved true in the case of Kurdish forces in northern Iraq in 2014, but, in 2015, the Syrian Kurds achieved the most-notable headway against ISIL on the northern border of Syria. The limited ISR assets also exacerbated the constant competition between targeting needs in Iraq versus Syria. The senior military commanders maintained a focus on preparing for a

---

[3] U.S. House of Representatives, Committee on Armed Services, 2015b. In his prepared statement, Secretary Carter said

> Next, in full coordination with the Government of Iraq, we're deploying a specialized expeditionary targeting force to assist Iraqi and Kurdish Peshmerga forces and to put even more pressure on ISIL. These special operators will over time be able to conduct raids, free hostages, gather intelligence, and capture ISIL leaders. That creates a virtuous cycle of better intelligence, which generates more targets, more raids, and more momentum. The raids in Iraq will be done at the invitation of the Iraqi government and focused on defending its borders and building the ISF's own capacity. This force will also be in a position to conduct unilateral operations into Syria.

[4] LTG James L. Terry served as the commanding general of the Combined Joint Task Force–Operation Inherent Resolve until September 2015, when he was succeeded by LTG Sean McFarland.

Mosul counteroffensive even though Iraq lacked both the capacity and will to tackle that daunting objective. After the fall of Ramadi in May 2015, and the effort to retake it stalled for many months, it gradually became clear that no counteroffensive in Mosul would be in the offing. Defense Intelligence Agency director LtGen. Vincent Stewart testified in March 2016 that he did not foresee a counteroffensive in Mosul in 2016, because of the ongoing battles to secure Anbar, and cut off that link between Mosul and Raqqa.[5]

Second, the U.S. coalition effort to build capacity, advise, and provide air support to partner forces in Iraq was far more modest and circumscribed than is generally understood. Roughly 3,400 to 3,870 U.S. troops were deployed in Iraq, plus approximately 2,000 coalition troops. The close attention to keeping troop numbers down impeded some efficiencies and effectiveness. The plan to train ten brigades touches only a fraction of the fighting forces. For force-protection reasons, the advisory effort was particularly constrained in terms of the geographic distribution, the units engaged, and the echelon at which advice was provided. In the first year, the train-and-equip effort for the Iraqi army entailed the training of six understrength Iraqi brigades and three Kurdish brigades at bases in Taji, Al Asad, Besmaya, and Irbil, as well as the special operations base. By March 2016, eight brigade sets of equipment had been delivered. HMMWVs and other vehicles would be delivered as U.S. production capacity permitted. U.S. and coalition forces also were providing advisory assistance to two combined joint operations centers in Baghdad and Irbil, at the CTS headquarters, at the Iraqi Ground Forces Command, and at the Taji depots, as well as at three operational commands in Baghdad and Anbar and Kurdistan.

In June, after the fall of Ramadi, U.S. advisers already in Iraq were permitted to deploy to Al-Taqaddum Air Base in eastern Anbar. Other requests to provide additional advisers to forward commands and units were not approved. In late 2015, the U.S. government announced that it would send 50 U.S. advisers to assist the Syrian opposition forces and an expeditionary targeting task force to Iraq to carry out joint

---

[5] U.S. House of Representatives, Committee on Armed Services, "Hearing: World Wide Threats," Washington, D.C.: CQ Transcriptions, March 2, 2016.

raids with Iraqi special operations units. As of March 2016, U.S. Central Command had forwarded additional requests to the Pentagon for advise-and-assist teams, human intelligence, and logistic support.[6]

Third, the Syria Train and Equip program was a modest effort that aimed for quality over quantity. It was not coordinated with any of the other military efforts the United States was pursuing in Syria. The train-and-equip effort suffered above all from the vetting criteria imposed, which limited the number of recruits, and it was further atomized through a scheme to train fighters in various locations. Finally, the U.S. government did not offer clear commitments that it would support these fighters once fielded. In August 2015, the first 54 fighters fielded in the heavily contested northwest came under immediate attack by ANF. The U.S. coalition provided air cover in that case, galvanizing a U.S. decision that had been long in coming to provide defensive support to troops it had trained. The program did not permit the U.S. advisers to accompany forces into Syria to provide field-advisory support, including logistics, intelligence, or operational planning assistance to the deployed units. The program was subsequently suspended when leaders of the NSF were captured by ANF, leaving just a handful of deployed NSF. After much hand-wringing, the decision was made to employ trainees to support other already-constituted forces in Syria. As for the Syrian Kurds, the United States provides air support to YPG movements targeting ISIL, but the U.S. forces were not permitted to train or equip the YPG for the first year of the effort.

The overall effects of the first 18 months of the military campaign can be summarized as follows:

U.S. efforts to bolster counter-ISIL forces yielded modest results. The advisory effort was circumscribed by location, unit, and function, and much of it was focused on vetting targets for air strikes rather than strategic and operational planning and advising. The training effort was also limited: Some 20,000 Iraqi army and *Peshmerga* forces had been trained by early 2016, including 2,000 CTS person-

---

[6]   U.S. Senate, Committee on Armed Services, "Hearing: United States Central Command, Africa Command, and United States Special Operations Command," Washington, D.C.: Federal News Service, March 8, 2016.

nel.[7] Equipping efforts also lagged. While U.S. and coalition officials made enormous efforts to rush equipment to Iraq, the U.S. processes and availability of materiel resulted in shortages of critical items. In particular, current the capacity of U.S. manufacturing production lines limited deliveries of armored vehicles and heavy weaponry. The enlistment and some arming of Sunni tribes appeared to be accelerating somewhat as of midyear. In Syria, the U.S. government eventually pledged air support to protect forces it has trained, but the small force was decimated and eventually turned into a support element for other units.

In terms of territory, the two notable battlefield advances were the KSF retaking of territory in northern Iraq in 2014 and the YPG's notable expansion of territory in northern Syria in 2015. The retaking of Tikrit was aided by ISIL's tactical withdrawal to reattack Baiji and Anbar. The battle for Baiji and the nearby oil refinery complex was drawn out, with CTS, Iraqi Army, and Federal Police forces eventually capturing those locations as Iraqi Shia militias moved south to besiege Fallujah.

However, the ISF showed notable advances during the eventual operation to reclaim Ramadi after months of dithering. The retaking of Ramadi in December 2015 was a critical victory that boosted the morale of the ISF and breathed new confidence into the struggling government. With U.S. training and assistance, the CTS and Iraqi Army brigades held combined arms maneuvers to include erecting a bridge during combat and using armored bulldozers to clear mines and create protective berms that facilitated assault into the city. Troops also used lines charges to clear minefields.

---

[7] By February 2016, 20,000 Iraqi troops had been trained. Five brigades were trained by the U.S.-led coalition in the first half of 2015. The 71st Brigade departed after the Al Asad Air Base was attacked and its leader killed; it did not complete training or receive equipment. It was subsequently assigned to the Baghdad Operations Command. The 72nd, 73rd, 75th, 76th, and 92nd Brigades completed training, although not all of their battalions went through the combined arms, live-fire breaching graduation exercise that was designed to simulate the full array of combat conditions and capabilities. The two Kurdish brigades were in training at three sites.

This success came at a high price. Heavy aerial bombardment and air support devastated some 80 percent of Ramadi, similar to the large-scale destruction in Kobani and Sinjar. The heavy use of airpower was in part because of the dug-in ISIL forces which had heavily mined and fortified the approaches to the city, built underground tunnels, and interior passages among the densely built city's homes. Estimates of the cost to rebuild the city after the long siege and eventual liberation reach $10 billion. (This suggests that a more unconventional approach to retaking Mosul may be warranted, as that city is home to up to a million people, and ISIL forces have created even more formidable defenses to include an intricate network of tunnels and berms.)

The U.S. air campaign resulted in 11,000 strikes that degraded but did not cripple ISIL operating capability and capacity. Several factors accounted for the relatively modest effectiveness achieved by the air campaign. First, restrictive rules of engagement were adopted in an effort to avoid civilian casualties. Second, most of the sorties were flown without a predetermined target (known as *dynamic targeting*). The top priority established by U.S. Central Command (CENTCOM) was to provide air support to forces in the field; therefore they would launch in anticipation of emergent targets. Targets did not always emerge or did not fall within the rules of engagement. Therefore, 65 percent of the total sorties between August 2014 and June 2015 returned with their ordnance.[8] The long distance between airfields in the Gulf and the Iraq and Syrian targets constituted another factor that affected the employment of airpower and limited the amount of airpower available at any given time.

Two other factors affecting the ability to identify targets are the amount of ISR assets available and the manner in which they are employed. The overall supply of ISR was limited, and the lack of dispersed U.S. ground forces limited intelligence collection. Other operations, such as those in Afghanistan, continue to claim a portion of the

---

[8] Secretary Carter provided these statistics in testimony, and Chairman of the Joint Chiefs of Staff Martin E. Dempsey added that the total rate of 65 percent of aircraft returning to base with ordnance was actually higher than the 83 percent rate in Afghanistan during a similar period of the conflict in 2012. See Carter, 2015c.

U.S. stock of drones that are in high demand for surveillance and strike missions. Persistent ISR coverage is necessary to track and positively identify high-value targets. Finally, another issue was the speed of the decisionmaking regarding airstrikes, which Prime Minister Abadi and others regarded as too slow. Factors affecting the decision time include the procedures used to positively identify targets, the communications equipment used by the Iraqi troops (or YPG in Syria), and the limited number of commands authorized to approve strikes, which creates a longer chain of approval.

Achieving Effects Through the Partnered Approach

Relying on indigenous forces to fight and win wars requires strategic patience and a concerted enabling effort. The weaker the forces, the more support and time will be required. Thus, a sufficiently robust effort, tailored to remedy the capability gaps and address the threat, will be required to build the indigenous capability and support its operations through a range of advisory functions. Insufficient emphasis on training, advice, and assistance can result in a vacuum created by too few troops and police forces to secure cleared areas. In addition, advisory efforts will achieve fewer lasting results if they focus too much on tactical combat formations to the detriment of leadership and command and control functions as well as the combat service and combat-service support functions required to provide key enablers and maintain the fighting force. Generally, U.S. and coalition advisers involved in the counter-ISIL campaign emphasized the need for ministerial-, command-, and operational-level advisory assistance down to the brigade level as the most important functions—not the tactical-level advisory support often mentioned in press reports. The forward-observer function for close air support can be provided through a variety of innovative techniques, and in any case, training indigenous forward observers is a more sustainable solution.

The United States and coalition experience since 2003 in training, equipping, advising, and assisting the CTS, Iraq's SOF, offers a useful model that can inform the wider effort. The U.S. and allied SOF provided intensive mentorship throughout the development of Iraq's SOF, from designing the selection process and training courses at Area Four, the CTS training base, to going into battle alongside them as combat advisers for years until the 2011 withdrawal of U.S. forces. The U.S. also focused on brigade and higher-command echelons in their advisory and training activities, mentoring the general officers in their interactions with the rest of the Iraqi defense establishment. The intensive partnering effort paid off in the most competent force in the Iraqi forces and the most integrated force of Shia, Sunni, and Kurds. The commanding general, Taleb al-Kenani, is a Shia, but he strongly upholds the diversity and professionalism for which the force has become known. Al-Kenani also enjoys the confidence of Prime Minister Abadi, and has served as the commander of the Combined Joint Operations Command overseeing the entire counter-ISIL campaign.

One very important flaw in Iraq's special-operations architecture has hampered the CTS, the counter-ISIL campaign, and the institutional development of Iraq's security forces. The decision in 2006 to create a freestanding CTS organization—and not make it part of the Ministry of Defense—created years of unnecessary frictions, competition, and budget uncertainty (as the CTS lacks of a standing line item in the budget).[9] Some U.S. mentors previously endorsed this model as comparable to the U.S. model, but even U.S. SOF are highly dependent on the services' budget except for SOF-unique equipment and other requirements. Creating an effective operational-command structure that effectively employs all of Iraq's forces is vital to achieving success against ISIL, as no one force has the capability to conduct the complex urban clearing and security operations that lie ahead.

Training

The effort to train ISF has been limited primarily by too few Iraqis showing up at the training centers. Most of the available personnel have been deployed in combat. Recruiting efforts have been insufficient, and many volunteers have flocked instead to the PMF. Some commanders have been reluctant to fill "ghost-soldier" slots that pro-

---

[9] Robinson, 2008, pp. 156, 164–166.

vide them extra funds, and a budget deficit because of low oil prices constrains the government's ability to expand the force. Consolidation of understrength units into fewer divisions will also require reducing the number of officers. The CTS recruiting effort is on track and will replenish the force by early 2016, to the assigned level of 11,000, a number that includes 14 forward observers trained to call in airstrikes.

The Syria Train and Equip program adapted its procedures based on its experience with the first classes with an eye to increasing throughput in the latter half of 2015. The program had focused on quality over quantity, adopting a model used to form the Afghan Local Police. Its framers suggested that it was not intended to serve as the primary fighting force, but instead to defend local areas and target key nodes of the ISIL support infrastructure. Another issue limiting the program's impact was the inability to pull entire units out of Syria, as they were engaged in fighting and commanders were reluctant to lose that combat power.

Equipping

On the U.S. side, the pace of equipping ISF has been primarily a function of (1) the length of time that security assistance packages require to move through all of the required processes and (2) the production capacity of U.S. manufacturers.[10] The U.S. government has sought to mitigate those delays by facilitating donations from coalition members and the transfer of U.S. excess defense articles and presidential drawdown authority. As a result, the ISF and KSF have ample small arms and ammunition and even stocks of antitank weapons. Although the Kurdistan Regional Government states that the government of Iraq has not provided arms, coalition and bilateral donations have provided significant materiel to the KSF.[11] Because of production-capacity limitations, armored vehicles are a particular area of shortfall, as well as

---

[10] U.S. security-assistance processes are not designed to support wartime operations. Advisers lacked timely supplies of training ammunition and smoke grenades. A security force assistance package needs to be developed for speedy delivery. In addition, commanders require small amounts of funds to be used for emergent needs.

[11] Data supplied by the U.S. Embassy Office of Security Cooperation-Baghdad in 2015.

M2 .50 caliber, 240B, and M249 weapons. The ISF lacks armored HMMWVs, 2,300 of which were lost in Mosul alone to ISIL forces, which employed them to great effect to breach fortifications and deliver vehicle-borne IEDs.[12] In May, the United States notified the ISF that 35 mine-resistant, ambush-protected vehicles were ready for delivery, but recommended that they be reserved for use in Mosul. In Syria, the United States provided equipment to the NSF, the FSA, and previous elements, such as Harakat Hazm, which received antitank TOW missiles. (Harakat Hazm was attacked by ANF and disbanded in 2015.)[13]

Advising

The advisory effort in Iraq has been constrained by force-protection concerns and other considerations. Prolonged internal debate occurred over the desired locations and echelon of the advisory effort. With the decision in June 2015 to move advisers into Al-Taqaddum Air Base in Anbar, the U.S.-led coalition now has advisers at two bases in Anbar and at several locations in Baghdad and Kurdistan. Other advisers provided virtual support through cell phones and ISR to other units. Such virtual advising was inadequate to achieve the necessary degree of coordination among disparate forces. The lack of coordination among Iraqi army, police, and CTS was in evidence during the fall of Ramadi in May 2015; the presence of U.S. advisers at the Anbar Operations Command or with the CTS First Brigade might have forestalled or mitigated this outcome.

GEN Martin Dempsey, at the time chairman of the Joint Chiefs of Staff, testified on several occasions that he had not recommended the use of forward observers or joint-terminal air controllers. He explained that he envisioned ultimately using advisers at the tactical level on a discrete time-limited basis.[14] "What I have recommended is that if we

---

[12] Haider Al-Abadi, 2015.

[13] Raja Abdulrahim, "U.S.-Backed Rebel Group in Syria Disbands," *Wall Street Journal*, March 1, 2015.

[14] See, for example, Ashton B. Carter, *Hearing to Receive Testimony in Review of the Defense Authorization Request for Fiscal Year 2016 and the Future Years Defense Program*, transcript of the United States Committee on Armed Services before the United States Senate, Wash-

find a unit which is led and is responsive and has an offensive mission where we can enable them or increase their likelihood of success, that I will make that recommendation," he testified. "But to restore or to put embedded advisers in on a habitual basis, the environment is just simply not set to do that."[15] This is an extremely narrow conception of advisory functions, and one whose narrowness limits their potential effectiveness. Inserting advisers into tactical units immediately prior to offensive combat operations does not provide the opportunity to train, plan, and prepare with those forces, much less influence their practices. Most U.S. advisory missions, particularly those carried out by SOF, have been long-term efforts spanning a range of functions that aim at professional-capable forces and operational results. The difference in the two conceptions of the advisory role is that of a narrow technical function versus a sustained advisory relationship based on trust that, ideally, ultimately instills a high degree of ethical professionalism, or, at a minimum, exercises sufficient influence to deter bad decisions and abusive actions. The objective is to achieve operational-level results that are ultimately sustainable by the indigenous forces operating independently. U.S. SOF applied this intensive mentoring model with the CTS forces from their inception, which is partly the reason for their higher level of competence. The same model was applied in developing Afghan SOF over the past decade.

Employing the Full Range of Advisory Functions

While the training and equipping of the ISF faces significant obstacles to acceleration, the use of advisers could be expanded dramatically. One issue involved in this decision is determining the specific functions advisers would play, at what echelons, and for what duration. The second issue is the assessment of risk to forces, and whether the risk to advisers can be mitigated to a sufficient degree, either through uni-

---

ington, D.C.: Alderson Reporting Company, March 3, 2015a; Ashton B. Carter, "Defense Department Fiscal Year 2016 Budget Request," testimony before the United States Senate Appropriates Subcommittee on Defense, C-SPAN.org, May 6, 2015b; Carter, 2015c; and U.S. House of Representatives, Committee on Armed Services, "Hearing: U.S. Policy and Strategy in the Middle East," Washington, D.C.: Federal News Service, June 17, 2015.

[15] See Carter, 2015c.

lateral force-protection measures and counterintelligence or through understandings reached with Iraqi and/or Iranian entities to target ISIL and not each other.

The U.S. debate has focused heavily on just one function: the placement of forward observers or joint terminal attack coordinators in tactical units to direct U.S. air strikes against enemy forces. Currently, Iraqi units place a call (usually with unsecured cell phones) to their commanders and U.S. advisers to request air support or to identify targets. A sometimes lengthy process then ensues to determine the geographic coordinates of the troops, other friendly forces, and the intended target, as well as whether civilians are in the vicinity.

Advisory functions at the operational and tactical level entail far more than just calling in close air support or assisting in the provision of other fires such as artillery. Advisers often perform a multitude of functions that include assessing forces' capability gaps based on observation of their operations; assisting in planning, intelligence collection, and analysis; facilitating communication and coordination with other units; supporting information operations; and reaching out to local populations through civil military and humanitarian operations. Colocation with units also enables advisers to identify and mitigate corruption, abuses, and sectarian behavior.

The experience of the NSF also underlined the importance of providing operational advisory assistance in addition to training and equipment. For much of the past year, the U.S. government refrained from specifying the types of advisory and enabling support it was prepared to provide to the Syrian opposition forces it trained and equipped. Although the U.S. government deemed it had the authority to train forces to attack ISIL, it hesitated in determining the legality of retaliating against Syrian government forces that interfered with those forces. When the NSF were inserted and came under attack, the United States did supply air support. The attack provided stark evidence of the need to provide fires—as well as logistics, intelligence, and other support—to a nascent force. This support can be supplied in some cases without placing U.S. advisers on the ground with tactical units. While current conditions may not permit placing advisers on the ground in Syria, the establishment of safe zones may provide such a platform.

To summarize, advisory functions play a critical role in translating capabilities into concrete performance and thus ensuring the policy's objective of a lasting defeat of ISIL. Training and equipping forces without a follow-on effort to support them in operations may risk mission failure. The support provided to Syrian opposition forces in the field has been extremely limited. The advisory function in Iraq was thinly staffed and not widely dispersed; in addition, many of the U.S. and coalition personnel at the Iraqi higher commands were primarily occupied with supporting the strike cells' targeting effort in support of the air campaign.

While field commanders sought a more-robust advisory role, in formulating his advice during most of the counter-ISIL campaign's first year, Dempsey appeared to rank "risk to forces" over "risk to mission." Although he appeared to be reluctant to advocate a more-robust advisory role in 2014, Dempsey had himself led sustained advisory efforts that had achieved effects even in adverse conditions with poorly trained, heavily politicized sectarian forces. As the commander of the Multi-National Security Transition Command–Iraq in 2007–2008, Dempsey personally led the effort to "reblue" the problematic Iraqi police forces, an effort that achieved considerable gains in weeding out poor or sectarian police and retraining others.[16] In one of his final appearances before Congress, he appeared to have shifted his position. Dempsey acknowledged the wide range of benefits that advisers provide and predicted that the June 2015 deployment of advisers to Al-Taqaddum would have a significant impact. "So our presence in the Anbar Operations Center is allowing the ISF to take a more deliberate campaign approach," he testified. "This is very much helping them understand the threat and formulate a campaign to address it so that they get credit for it and they become credible to the people of al-Anbar province."[17]

---

[16] Robinson, 2008, pp. 154, 336.

[17] Carter, 2015c.

CHAPTER FIVE

Recommendations

The gains shown by the accelerating military counter-ISIL campaign in the latter part of 2015 indicates that the partnered approach to defeating ISIL is indeed viable if sufficient allied support is provided as Iraqi and Syrian capacity grows and strengthens. This course appears to provide greater prospects of success with fewer risks and costs than the other two main alternatives (of large-scale U.S. military intervention or containment focused on airstrikes and support to neighboring countries). Increasing the scale and effectiveness of the campaign through a comprehensive advisory effort is relatively straightforward, but it will take time. The building of competent forces will not occur overnight. However, the lasting defeat of ISIL will not occur through military measures alone. It will require addressing the political impediments in Iraq and Syria in a concerted and sustained manner. Articulating the political aspects of the counter-ISIL strategy in concrete terms and adequately resourcing them is therefore paramount.

This political line of effort should be seen as the foundation of a successful strategy and become a top priority for the U.S. government. A major effort will be needed to support Prime Minister Abadi and help forge a coalition, including major Shia figures, around the key needed points of consensus:

- decentralization of government according to Iraq's law and constitution
- integration and eventual demobilization of militias
- a basic compact built on the understanding that all benefit from arrangements to resolve disputes with the Kurdish regional gov-

ernment and allow for peaceful coexistence of the Shia majority and substantial Sunni minority.

Finally, the political and military components of the strategy must be synchronized to create the leverage and sustain the commitments required for success. Military aid can directly encourage political compromise, and political progress will enormously strengthen the will of the population to continue fighting ISIL. The following detailed recommendations posit measures to achieve the three goals of a more-robust and effective partnered military campaign, political reconciliation in both Iraq and Syria, and greater synchronization of the political-military aspects of the strategy.

Recommendations for Improving the Military Line of Effort

The weakness of the ISF will not be remedied in the short term, and many of the other forces' limitations are also not easily overcome. While none of the existing forces working alone can hope to degrade and defeat ISIL, however, a coordinated effort among all of them might succeed, as the battlefield successes in late 2015 and early 2016 showed. The United States could take several steps to improve the efficacy of such a coordinated effort, as well as to mitigate the risks and problematic aspects of this less-than-ideal arrangement. The urgency of gaining more traction in the counter-ISIL campaign—and the lack of any more palatable alternative to do so—is the principal argument in favor of this course.

Senior U.S. officials have made more frequent and visible trips to Baghdad, which is an important symbol and means to achieve greater coordination and influence in Iraq. While the United States does not enjoy a position of uncontested and primary influence in Baghdad, it does have enormous military, economic, financial, and diplomatic leverage that it can bring to bear. Its previous posture of limited and cautious support did not yield significant results. An arm's length approach may have worked to undermine rather than strengthen Prime

Minister Abadi and produce the desired concessions from more intransigent and sectarian actors. The measures recommended in this chapter would be undertaken with the support of Prime Minister Abadi.

The key elements of a more robust and more expeditious partnered approach in Iraq are:

- a more robust, empowered, and geographically distributed U.S. advisory presence that fulfills a range of functions, to include assisting operational commands, combat advising with trusted units, and coordinating among a wide variety of anti-ISIL forces. Quick-reaction forces, medical evacuation, and intelligence enablers will be needed, for a total of several thousand additional troops
- expedited delivery of urgently needed equipment to ISF, including urgent CTS needs; a more dispersed advisory model should improve ISF performance and reduce previous losses of equipment to enemy forces
- a long-term train-and-equip program for the ISF and the police that is conditioned on the Iraqi government's commitment to enlist 30,000 Sunnis into the security forces or government-sponsored mobilization force, coupled with an agreed pathway for institutionalization or demobilization of all militias in accordance with the Iraqi constitution, which bans militias
- an unconventional warfare component that recruits and employs Sunnis who reject ISIL to conduct information operations; gather intelligence; build an underground organization in ISIL-held areas; and target and sabotage ISIL forces, equipment, and installations.[1]

In Syria, the elements of a more robust and efficacious partnered approach would include the following efforts:

---

[1] DoD's *Dictionary of Military and Associated Terms* defines unconventional warfare as "activities conducted to enable a resistance movement or insurgency to coerce, disrupt, or overthrow a government or occupying power by operating through or with an underground, auxiliary, and guerrilla force in a denied area." (See Director for Joint Force Development, *Department of Defense Dictionary of Military and Associated Terms*, Joint Publication 1-02, Washington, D.C.: Pentagon, November 8, 2010, as amended through June 15, 2015.)

- Reenergize diplomatic efforts to seek a transitional regime in Syria in concert with NATO and regional allies, while forging a common strategy among those allies to increase military pressure on the Assad regime and to protect moderate Syrian opposition forces from Russian airstrikes. Russian actions create an opportunity for a new consensus among anti-Assad forces. A united front may eventually persuade Russia and Iran that the costs of sustaining the Assad regime will only continue to mount, and that their interests are better served by supporting a political transition.
- Assist or support other countries' assistance to Syrian opposition groups that are not affiliated with al Qaeda and adopt less-constrained vetting criteria for Syrian opposition fighters that accepts their interest in fighting the Assad regime. This support should, at a minimum, include antitank and anti-aircraft missiles if the coalition is unwilling to provide air support to protect the forces from Russian airstrikes.
- Encourage Syrian opposition forces to unite to attack ISIL as part of their offensive, providing additional support to those groups that do so.

In both countries, a more effective air campaign could be achieved by adopting these additional measures:

- increasing the emphasis on intelligence-driven targeting enabled by additional ISR assets, human intelligence, sensitive site exploitation, and all-source intelligence analysts—without abandoning the commitment to avoid civilian casualties
- speeding the targeting process by delegating target-engagement authority, enabling Iraqi and Syrian forward observers through better equipment and training, and as necessary, to selectively employ coalition forward observers.

Resource a Robust Advisory Effort at the Operational Level

The main effort should be focused on advising units in operations and in coordinating among the widely disparate forces, despite their limitations and flaws. This means more advisers in more locations undertaking more functions—with all of the available and willing partners. A more expedient approach is needed in the short term to gain traction and generate momentum. Virtual advising is an inadequate formula. There are indications that the Iraqi government will embrace a more robust advisory effort to include additional combat advising—which is not the same as deploying combat brigades to assume the major role in the fighting.

Deploying advisers to area commands and to trusted CTS and other units could, if taken in combination with other measures, have significant effect in reversing ISIL gains. These advisers should be permitted to perform the full range of advisory functions as described in the previous section. The much-needed coordination of plans and operations among army, police, CTS, and tribal forces can only occur at these lower levels. The advisers' dispersed presence would allow them to gain much greater situational awareness of the partner units' strengths and weaknesses, as well as of enemy positions. The ability to communicate with and assess potential tribal recruits is another advantage. While some selected tactical-level advising may be warranted, a great deal of effect can be achieved by enabling indigenous forces to more accurately mark their positions and communicate more securely and rapidly. U.S. SOF have identified the Exelis satellite radio, already in U.S. Army stocks, as a suitable, easy-to-use option. Advisers should also be permitted to assist fielded Syrian opposition forces with logistics, intelligence, and operational advice from relatively secure command posts—or, if and when conditions permit—in the field.

These steps entail the acceptance of higher levels of risk to U.S. forces. That decision is one of policy, but many commanders favor a measured assumption of greater risk, as it will hasten and increase the effects sought by the policy. The lack of more-concerted progress in the Arab areas of the Iraq and Syria battlefield threaten to entrench ISIL rule ever more deeply and harden the cities' defenses against both frontal and subversive operations. At present in Iraq, the CTS and KSF units may be the only tactical units where U.S. combat advisers should be placed. The issue of combat advisers has taken on outsize importance in many media accounts. It is even more important that advisers advise and assist at operational- and national-level commands to ensure a coherent campaign and coordinated use of the units in the field.

The successes achieved in Kurdistan are because of the capability of the Kurdish forces as well as the ability of U.S. advisers to move with the sector/brigade command to forward locations. The risk is much lower because of the existence of a relatively fixed and secure forward line, so decisions about moving advisers into tactical units should only be made where the Iraqi unit is deemed capable and sufficient air support and backup is available. Many of those advocating extensive use of tactical combat advising are likely unaware of how much less secure the Iraqi environment is today compared with 2003–2010.

The various Shia militias are playing significant roles on the battlefield, and the chief requirement for greater coordination with these groups is a risk-mitigation strategy that would include an explicit understanding that U.S. advisers will not be targeted and that the response to violating that understanding would be swift and overwhelming. At the same time, the United States can improve its familiarity with the Shia groups and actors to determine whether productive relationships with some of them are possible. The groups most closely aligned with Iran and most antagonistic to the United States (e.g., KH and AAH) likely warrant vigilance rather than cooperation. But to achieve the desired anti-ISIL effects, the joint task force commander should be permitted to explore the prospect of effective working relationships that serve U.S. and Iraqi interests. Just as some Sunni provincial officials and tribal leaders in Anbar and Salah al-Din have recognized, the exigencies of the crisis warrant such marriages of convenience that may turn out to be the pathway to a reunified state.

There is, of course, no guarantee that a robust advisory effort would produce the desired results, given the fragmented array of partners and the complex political environment that includes an intra-Shia Iraqi power struggle, anti-American Shia militias, and Iran's desire to exert maximum influence. But the United States has superior materiel and resources, and Iraqis within and outside the government have repeatedly voiced their desire for greater U.S. support.

U.S. advisers successively supported partner forces previously in Iraq, and as part of this effort, U.S. advisers very intensively supported the CTS and interior ministry's emergency response forces for about eight years. In this mode, U.S. forces were operating as combat advisers with tactical units but also with brigade, division, and national-level commands. As noted above, Afghanistan also adopted this model. In the Philippines, a different model was applied. U.S. SOF provided direct support, including ISR, medical evacuation, and other support, but the U.S. advisers were barred from combat; they provided this operational advisory assistance during operations at the brigade level and were permitted to move to the brigade commanders' forward tactical command posts. The guidance commonly given for this type of direct support advising is that advisers remain "one terrain feature away" from the combat. They must have good battlefield intelligence to determine the location of the last position of "cover and concealment." The Philippines model, which permitted U.S. advisers to be armed and to fire in self-defense, may be applicable to the Iraqi case. The U.S. advisory support provided in Colombia over more than a decade to multiple military and police units at all echelons was another case of successful advisory functions excluding a combat role. In some cases, the United States has restricted the advisory function to focus narrowly on counterterrorism units, or exclusively on tactical formations, rather than the entire gamut of military capabilities required. These cases have generally been less successful.[2]

These examples illustrate the track record of U.S. advisory efforts. Obviously, Iraq is a far more lethal environment, and advisers dispersed to multiple bases clearly would require additional support personnel to provide air support, medical evacuation, forward surgical teams, quick-reaction forces, and additional intelligence capabilities. A detailed troop-to-task analysis and risk assessment would be needed to determine the force level required for an appropriately robust and supported advisory mission. As a rough estimate, it would require some additional thousands of troops, though probably less than 10,000.

---

[2] These observations are drawn from several RAND studies, including Linda Robinson, Patrick B. Johnston, and Gillian Oak, *U.S. Special Operations Forces in the Philippines, 2001–2014*, Santa Monica, Calif.: RAND Corporation, RR-1236-OSD, 2016.

Iraq does not lack in talented generals: Abdul Amir al-Shammari, the commander of the Baghdad Operations Command, is one of them, along with al-Kenani. While it is understandable that Iraqi officials wish to ensure the security of Baghdad, and rely on Iraq's professional military rather than sectarian militias or police to do so, the large amount of forces held in reserve in the Baghdad Command hampered the first year and a half of the war effort. To adequately staff a robust and distributed advisory effort, would probably require some additional thousands of troops, depending on the level of force protection and support units required. In no case would a robust advisory effort approach the numbers needed for a U.S. combat mission. The decision to allow U.S. SOF to engage in joint raids with Iraqi and Kurdish SOF should not be a prelude to U.S. infantry units assuming frontline combat roles. That course likely would inhibit the needed development of Iraqi fighting and leadership skills, and quite possibly spark negative reactions from sectors of Iraqi society.

Increase the Effectiveness of the Air Campaign

The coalition air campaign can be enhanced through the use of additional assets, an emphasis on deliberate targeting, and several measures to increase the speed and accuracy of the targeting cycle—all without sacrificing the laudable goal of avoiding civilian casualties. A more intelligence-driven approach to the war will, out of necessity, require more ISR assets, as well as more intelligence analysts. The way in which the increased pool of assets is employed should also be shifted to focus on deliberate targeting. This may produce fewer strikes, but they would be of higher value. The measures of effectiveness should not be simply the number of fighters killed or the number of buildings or tanks hit, but whether actions cripple the organization's ability to command, control, and sustain its operations. Some amount of dynamic targeting is required, and the opening of Turkey air bases to armed strikes will greatly increase the amount of time aircraft can spend on target. Close air support to fighting forces is important to maintain morale, but over time that function can ideally shift wholly to the Iraqis. The other way to increase effectiveness is to increase the ability of Iraqi and Syrian forces to quickly mark their positions and positively identify their targets. Equipment and training can facilitate this. Equipping units with satellite radios, as mentioned earlier, will speed the targeting process. Finally, designating additional target-engagement authorities to verify the targeting procedures and approve air strikes can speed the approval process. In some cases, coalition-forward observers may be warranted, provided they are with trusted units, but the goal should be to enable indigenous forces as quickly as possible.

Commit to a Long-Term Train-and-Equip Program

In Iraq, the only hedge against the growing power of Shia militias backed by Iran is the building of a professional security force. Duly constituted ISF should absorb appropriately vetted tribal and militia forces. Regardless of the future boundaries of the Iraqi state, a professional and capable ISF with strong U.S. ties can contribute to regional stability. Security sector reforms must be part of this program to address transparency and accountability issues, as well as to resolve the chronic frictions between the defense ministry and the CTS.

The United States should support Prime Minister Abadi and all nonsectarian elements with public demonstrations of support, expedited arms, and long-term commitments to fulfill the terms of the Strategic Framework Agreement.[3] Only a robust and concrete program of military, political, and economic support will signal U.S. intent to compete with Iran for influence in Iraq. Such a commitment should include support for development of a consensus among the major political blocs to prevent an entrenched militia structure whose military and political power will undermine the central Iraqi government. The long-term regional and global interests of Iraqi Shia are best served by the development of relations with other centers of power in addition to Iran.

In return for this commitment of substantial support over the long term, the United States should seek a firm pledge of incorporating 40,000 Sunnis into the PMF and/or the security forces, as well as

---

[3]   See "Strategic Framework Agreement for a Relationship of Friendship and Cooperation Between the United States of America and the Republic of Iraq," U.S. Department of State, November 17, 2008.

a clear pathway for the PMF militia structure to demobilize or transition into duly-constituted security forces. Whether through creation of a national guard or by providing a greater local role in the recruitment and employment of a decentralized security force, as the Provincial Powers Law (Law 21, Article 31-10) appears to envision, some mechanism that allows Sunni-majority areas to protect themselves could allow the vision of a united but federal state to gain traction and sap strength from ISIL and the fence-sitters in the Sunni community.

Add a Significant Unconventional Effort to the Counter-ISIL Campaign

The focus on training and equipping forces sufficiently robust to confront ISIL runs the risk of ignoring the unconventional aspects of the hybrid threat. First, an unconventional approach to recapturing Mosul and Raqqa would avoid the large-scale physical destruction and possible high casualties that would result from a conventional assault. Just as important, an unconventional warfare model can help guard against the prospect of defeating the ISIL proto-state only to confront a virulent ISIL 2.0 that relies on guerrilla and terrorist tactics to destabilize the region and extend its attacks from remaining safe havens. The Sunni population must form the core of any unconventional approach to unseating ISIL, through popular mobilization, formation of urban undergrounds, and campaigns of sabotage and assassination. These efforts can be supported through the raising of Sunni tribal militias under the PMF program, but they should be augmented by civil affairs and information operations designed to counter ISIL subjection of civilians and media operations at the local and provincial level. At a minimum, a more robust engagement with the Sunni tribes by U.S. and coalition forces is needed; U.S. special operations currently have limited subject-matter expert exchanges and work largely through the Iraqi government forces.

A successful unconventional effort could dramatically reduce the duration, human toll, and physical destruction of conventional urban operations to retake the provincial capitals of Mosul and Raqqa. The difficulties of mounting such an effort, however, should not be underestimated. The unparalleled brutality exhibited by ISIL against civilians and captured fighters shows the lengths to which they are prepared to go to intimidate and squelch any opposition. The massacre of some 700 members of the Shaitat tribe in Syria in August 2014 is one example of the atrocities that ISIL has committed with this objective. Anbar tribes have been decimated by similar acts. There is also the reality of active and passive cooperation with ISIL (and its predecessor) among the Sunni population. The former Baathist members of ISIL have excellent counterintelligence and other training to ferret out an underground resistance. Finally, most unconventional warfare efforts take years to mature and produce results.

Increase Coordination of and Support to Syrian Opposition Forces

If the U.S. government intends to pursue a successful strategy in Syria that relies on Syrian ground forces, it must adapt to a more realistic model that accepts the fact that Syrians want to fight Assad. The only way to reach the necessary mass of indigenous forces is to welcome those who will fight ISIL and to seek to unite all those forces as well as the various funding streams that are supporting them. The reality is that a loose alliance exists among all forces fighting Assad. Finally, the YPG has made effective gains, and cooperation among all effective opposition forces can produce synergies. The nascent FSA and YPG alliance should be encouraged, and the YPG can continue to take steps to assuage Syrian Sunni concerns through credible actions. Continuing a train-and-equip element to the program also has merit. While the Syria Train and Equip program did not explicitly have a long-term purpose, a well-trained and professional force can contribute to a permanent security institution for the state entity that survives the war. In essence, the vetting criteria of the Syria Train and Equip program made it a stillborn initiative—in particular, the requirement that trainees agree not to fight against the Assad regime. These steps to increase military pressure on Assad while simultaneously fighting ISIL should be coupled with a significant diplomatic push to remove Assad. While Russia appears committed to supporting Assad for the moment, this could change as time passes and the costs mount. It may also be that Iran would back a transitional regime in exchange for protections of Alawites and its corridor to Lebanon. Forging a united front with

NATO and regional allies will strengthen the U.S. hand in pursuing a force-backed diplomatic strategy.

Emphasize the Political Effort and Overall Synchronization of the Counter-ISIL Strategy

The following broad changes should be considered to enhance the overall approach and the implementation:

- The overall strategy to defeat ISIL would benefit from a comprehensive review based on a deep understanding of the drivers of ISIL's growth and expansion in Iraq and Syria and globally. Strategists and planners should envision a decadelong endeavor to achieve the conditions necessary for lasting defeat of ISIL.
- A detailed political strategy should be developed and implemented with the assistance of senior officials to underline the criticality of this element of the overall approach. A partnership with Iraq's government is needed, and a stronger and more effective coalition in Syria, to address core issues driving the conflict.
- The implementation of a revised strategy based on this understanding should be more robustly synchronized, particularly the political and military elements. Increased military aid should be explicitly tied to these critical understandings.

The U.S. counter-ISIL strategy has been implemented in a decentralized manner, rather than through a single entity charged with synchronizing the multiple lines of effort in the strategy. The Special Presidential Envoy to the Global Coalition to Counter ISIL, retired Gen. John R. Allen, and his successor Brett McGurk, were not charged with acting as the overall synchronizer of the U.S. effort. The envoy's mandate was rather to oversee the global coalition of 66 countries align coalition members to colead efforts on some of the nine lines. In 2015, a National Security Council official, Robert Malley, was charged with overseeing the interagency coordination of the various U.S. departments and agencies assigned roles in executing the nine lines of the strategy. Secretary Carter testified that he and Secretary of State John Kerry were performing the overall synchronization role, but given these cabinet officials' multiple duties, it is unlikely that their schedules would permit them to provide the type of intensive oversight and direct orchestration of both political and military efforts to achieve maximum effect on both fronts.

The next administration may consider the benefits of such overall orchestration by a dedicated official or office. Congress may also recommend designation of such a lead entity, along with a regular report on progress, as it did in the Iraq and Afghanistan wars, to compel some accounting of progress and shortfalls. Another issue is how the United States can manage a campaign that is rapidly turning into two campaigns: one focusing on the highly complex Iraq-Syria battlefield, and another addressing ISIL as it expands globally. The partnered approach to degrading and defeating ISIL on the ground would benefit from an increased effort to synchronize the lines of effort and to focus those lines on achieving some near-term progress that could lend momentum to the military effort. Achieving this synergy is the chief objective of a campaign.

The political and military lines of effort particularly would benefit from increased synchronization. As stated earlier, the objective of an inclusive Iraqi government is a difficult and long-term one. A major surge in the political line of effort is warranted. This should focus not just on Prime Minister Abadi, but on the major political blocs represented in parliament. Under the majoritarian system in which the Shia majority has the winning votes, the first priority should be to engage with the Shia parties and leaders, and the second priority to encourage the three separate Sunni blocs to come together on a vision for the proposed national guard or an alternative and, over the longer term, on a federalized system with greater decentralization.

Iraqi legislation is needed for two important objectives: to provide Sunnis with the ability to secure their own provinces and to provide a pathway to incorporate the temporary (and unconstitutional) militia and PMF into regular government security institutions, with appropriate vetting and retraining, to prevent the growth and entrenchment of permanent militia structures, as in Lebanon. If sufficient support cannot be found to pass the national guard legislation, other vehicles to accomplish these objectives should be explored. For example, it is possible that Article 31-10 of the revised provincial powers law could provide a vehicle for reaching a specific formula for sharing security responsibilities with the provinces. The U.S. government should strongly back movement toward the objectives and pledge sustained multiyear assistance for those security institutions to encourage Iraqis to coalesce around solutions of their own making.

Beyond the security-related issues, strong, visible, and concrete U.S. support for political compromises and government reforms will greatly improve the prospects for Prime Minister Abadi's success and the development of a positive vision for Iraq's future. While closure for the de-Baathification process does not appear to be possible at the moment, the parliament's action on the aforementioned provincial powers law indicates alacrity and responsiveness not seen in earlier sessions of parliament. Moreover, the provincial powers law includes an explicit formula for sharing oil revenues with the provinces ($5 petrodollars per barrel), which would resolve another obstacle in the path toward a more decentralized but still unitary Iraq; the oil-poor Sunni provinces would be guaranteed a stream of revenues, assuming the law is implemented. The plan for devolving eight ministries' functions largely to the provinces also will require implementation. Devolution of administrative responsibilities has been under way for some time with the support of the U.S. Agency for International Development, although that program is scheduled to end and would need to be extended to support the ambitious new law.

The U.S. government is not devoid of influence and is unmatched in its ability to bring economic resources, military hardware, and international influence to bear in assistance to Iraq. Yet the fact is that the U.S. voice is not necessarily the most influential one in Baghdad at this point. It may be that the diplomatic community in Baghdad can form a contact group to support the search for political compromises. In any event, Iraq's cleavages are deep will not be easily bridged. But Sunni views on acceptable solutions are evolving, and some nationalist Shia voices, including that of the controversial Muqtada al-Sadr, are seeking to forge cross-sectarian reform coalitions. The United States will benefit from much deeper engagement with the range of Shia parties to support the emergence of a constructive consensus among the majority of Iraqis. As part of this developing relationship, the United States should be sensitive to Iraqi prerogatives in directing the war effort and determining its operational priorities.

U.S. military officials understand that the success of military operations to unseat ISIL ultimately will depend on what happens after the combat phase. Yet the humanitarian line of effort is inadequately synchronized and under-resourced. This line of effort faces an enormous hurdle in coping with an unprecedented wave of Syrian and Iraqi refugees and internally displaced persons. The enormity of this task obscures the criticality, in military terms, of addressing certain locations. One positive sign is the return of most residents of Tikrit and the reopening of the university there. However, continued assistance to Sunni areas must be a high priority to inoculate them from ISIL recruitment. In the mixed province of Diyala and other areas, Shia militias have become an entrenched presence. Salah al-Din province occupies a critical crossroads between Mosul and Anbar and is the location of the country's largest oil refinery, now destroyed but still an area that ISIL would like to recapture. It is also the primary route to Baghdad, which will make it contested terrain so long as the war continues.

Finally, coalition members are not entirely aligned with the U.S. counter-ISIL strategy and a sharper effort is warranted to address particular gaps and contradictions. Although several Gulf countries are participating in the air campaign, these states' relatively weak roles are noteworthy. It should also be noted that Saudi Arabia has finally reopened its embassy in Baghdad. Given the Gulf states' concerns about Iraq's close ties with Iran, a consistent Iraqi outreach to those states would be needed to build ties of trust and cooperation that could temper Iran's influence in Baghdad.[4] In Syria, several coalition members reportedly are actively aiding jihadist groups in a bid to oust Assad. While one of those beneficiaries, ANF, has temporarily renounced intentions to attack Western targets, it remains an affili-

---

[4]   Mustafa al-Kadhimi, "Could Saudi-Iraqi Ties Be Key to Defeating Islamic State?" Al Monitor.com, October 9, 2015.

ate of al Qaeda. The U.S. goal should be to forge a consensus among the Gulf States and other regional partners over which groups should receive aid to avoid the pyrrhic outcome of radical Islamists coming to power in Syria.

The other glaring issue is the ongoing flow of foreign fighters and trade (including smuggled oil and looted artifacts) supporting ISIL, a symptom of the continued lax visa and border policies of Turkey. Turkey's priority has been to seek the ouster of Syria's Assad rather than shut off the flow of foreign fighters, but the attacks by ISIL in Turkish territory appeared to have prompted a reassessment. In any case, Turkey's recent decision to carry out airstrikes against ISIL and allow the coalition to do the same from its bases is welcome and may provide an opportunity to secure further measures to stem the flow of fighters and resources. The additional support Turkey has pledged to retake the remaining border area from ISIL is also promising, though its attacks on the PKK complicate efforts to build a unified Syrian ground force. If an effective coalition is to be forged, these substantial frictions among key U.S. allies require full-time attention at senior levels.

Conclusion

The United States has embarked on a course of supporting partners in a bid to defeat ISIL, an effort that it envisioned as requiring a minimum of three years. Events of the past 18 months indicate that given ISIL's resilience, the campaign will take quite a while longer. This evaluation suggests that much more can be achieved, however, with substantial revisions to the strategy.

The three primary changes needed are (1) a more-robust and comprehensive partnered approach, (2) a concrete political strategy, and (3) closer synchronization of political and military measures to gain maximum benefit from both. This course appears the most promising option of those available. The primary argument in favor of the extended effort implied by this course is that only indigenous ground forces can provide lasting security and stability to Iraq and Syria. The search for a political consensus among Iraqis and among Syrians is an equally difficult and time-consuming endeavor, but the costs that continuing internecine war—and the ripple effects for regional and international security—impose are enormous and appear to warrant this increased investment.

The two alternative strategies appear to carry higher costs and risks and do not promise substantially better outcomes. A large-scale U.S. military intervention would not supply the needed indigenous ground force to hold the territory, and the intervention would be costly in terms of both lives and treasure The counterproductive effects could be enormous—if indeed it could be implemented. The government of Iraq is not likely to accept a U.S. combat role or other unilateral actions. Even if it did, a large U.S. combat presence would almost certainly spur ISIL recruitment, possibly on an even more massive scale than seen to date, and spark nationalist opposition among ordinary Iraqis and Syrians.

The other alternative—a containment strategy—would also yield questionable benefits, although it would probably be the lowest-cost option available. This alternative would include a combination of continued attrition from the air and perhaps by SOF, coupled with greater support to neighboring countries such as Jordan to add a containment dimension.[5] In essence, it would be a standoff attempt at continued degradation. Such an approach would amount largely to "mowing the grass," however, and would not provide any endgame for the conflict. Given porous borders and a fluid enemy that already has global reach,

---

[5] See, for example, the version of "offensive containment" advocated by Cronin (Audrey Kurth Cronin, "ISIS Is Not a Terrorist Group: Why Counterterrorism Won't Stop the Latest Jihadist Threat," *Foreign Affairs*, February 16, 2015). and "an aggressive form of containment" by Fromson and Simon (James Fromson and Steven Simon, "ISIS: The Dubious Paradise of Apocalypse Now," *International Institute for Strategic Studies*, Vol. 57, No. 3, May 11, 2015, pp. 7–56). These proposals both resemble the current presidential administration approach more than a strict containment approach, but they aim rather at degrading than defeating ISIL. Cronin emphasizes increased high-level diplomatic measures, while Fromson and Simon argue that the military, political, ideological, and governance vulnerabilities will eventually cause its erosion and collapse. Posen (2015) advocated containment, but he did not describe the details of an approach that, he said, "could be achieved at bargain prices, with a low U.S. profile." (Barry R. Posen, "Prelude to a Quagmire: The Addition of 450 New U.S. Military Trainers to Iraq Is the Next Step Down a Slippery Slope," *Foreign Policy*, June 16, 2015.)

containment in practice may prove ineffective. The workability of a containment strategy is highly questionable, given the ISIL worldwide network and its demonstrated ability to wage multiple attacks in the heart of Europe. The largest migrant crisis since World War II is providing further fuel, as well as ample evidence of the porosity of borders and the effects of constant global communications. Finally, the cost of containment is not negligible. The administration requested $7.5 billion in its fiscal year 2017 budget request to Congress for continuing its counter-ISIL campaign in Iraq and Syria, a very large portion of that request is to replenish the stock of expensive precision munitions that would also be the mainstay of a containment strategy.

The most promising approach for achieving a lasting defeat of ISIL is through sufficient support to Iraqis and Syrians so they become the permanent "hold force" capable of preventing any resurgent threat. As this report has emphasized, the partners in this case are inadequate, limited, or problematic, but these deficits may be remediable if the strategy is adequately resourced and sustained.

The successful development and employment of the CTS gives reason to believe that robust, extended mentoring that includes selection criteria, training and equipping, and operational advising in the field at all echelons does work. The creation of a professional military is an important ingredient in creating a more-stable Iraq. The political challenges facing Iraqis are significant, but the choice the United States faces is whether to cede the field to Iran or invest in a partnership that can help stabilize the region. The path in Syria is less easy still, but without Syrians to stabilize their land, there is no future but war. The diplomatic efforts will not prosper without a willingness to confront those who wish to win by force. The correct endgame is a political solution, but it does not appear attainable without an astute blend of diplomacy and force, which calls for skilled statecraft indeed.

Selected Bibliography

al-Abadi, Haider, transcript of interview in a public forum with Dr. Jon B. Alterman, senior vice president, Zbigniew Brzezinski Chair in Global Security and Geostrategy, and director, Center for Strategic and International Studies, *Statesmen's Forum: Looking Forward: A Holistic Strategy for Iraq*, Washington, D.C.: Superior Transcripts LLC, April 16, 2015.

Abdulrahim, Raja, "U.S.-Backed Rebel Group in Syria Disbands," *Wall Street Journal*, March 1, 2015. As of October 6, 2015:
http://www.wsj.com/articles/u-s-backed-rebel-group-in-syria-disbands-1425253180

Agence France-Presse, "Iraqi PM Admits Expensive Loss of Humvees," *AlJazeera*, June 1, 2015. As of October 15, 2015:
http://www.aljazeera.com/news/2015/06/iraqi-pm-admits-expensive-loss-humvees-150601052521757.html

Biden, Joe, "Iraqis Must Rise Above Their Differences to Rout Terrorists," *Washington Post*, August 22, 2014. As of October 6, 2015:
https://www.washingtonpost.com/opinions/vice-president-biden-iraqis-can-rout-isil-by-rising-above-differences/2014/08/22/0dcfdc06-2a12-11e4-958c-268a320a60ce_story.html

Carter, Ashton B., *Hearing to Receive Testimony in Review of the Defense Authorization Request for Fiscal Year 2016 and the Future Years Defense Program*, transcript of the United States Committee on Armed Services before the United States Senate, Washington, D.C.: Alderson Reporting Company, March 3, 2015a. As of October 6, 2015:
http://www.armed-services.senate.gov/imo/media/doc/15-19%20-%203-3-15.pdf

———, "Defense Department Fiscal Year 2016 Budget Request," testimony before the United States Senate Appropriates Subcommittee on Defense, C-SPAN.org, May 6, 2015b. As of October 15, 2015:
http://www.c-span.org/video/?325804-1/
secretary-carter-general-dempsey-testimony-defense-departments-2016-budget

————, *Hearing to Receive Testimony on Counter-ISIL (Islamic State of Iraq and the Levant) Strategy*, transcript of the United States Committee on Armed Services before the United States Senate, Washington, D.C.: Alderson Reporting Company, July 7, 2015c. As of October 6, 2015:
http://www.armed-services.senate.gov/imo/media/doc/15-61%20-%207-7-15.pdf

Caspari, Sarah, "Air Force: ISIS Selfie Led to Its Headquarters Destruction," *Christian Science Monitor*, June 5, 2015. As of October 6, 2015:
http://www.csmonitor.com/USA/USA-Update/2015/0605/
Air-Force-ISIS-selfie-led-to-its-headquarters-destruction-video

Clapper, James, *Hearing to Receive Testimony on Worldwide Threats*, transcript of the U.S. Senate Armed Services Committee hearing, Washington, D.C.: Alderson Reporting Company, February 26, 2015. As of October 6, 2015:
http://www.armed-services.senate.gov/imo/media/doc/15-18%20-%202-26-15.pdf

Cronin, Audrey Kurth, "ISIS Is Not a Terrorist Group: Why Counterterrorism Won't Stop the Latest Jihadist Threat," *Foreign Affairs*, February 16, 2015. As of October 6, 2015:
https://www.foreignaffairs.com/articles/middle-east/2015-02-16/
isis-not-terrorist-group

DeYoung, Karen, and Missy Ryan, "Senior ISIS Leader Killed in U.S. Raid in Syria," *Washington Post*, May 16, 2015. As of October 6, 2015:
https://www.washingtonpost.com/world/national-security/us-kills-islamic-state-leader-in-syria-raid/2015/05/16/31280b26-fbca-11e4-a13c-193b1241d51a_story.html

Director for Joint Force Development, *Department of Defense Dictionary of Military and Associated Terms*, Joint Publication 1-02, Washington, D.C.: Pentagon, November 8, 2010, as amended through June 15, 2015.

Fromson, James, and Steven Simon, "ISIS: The Dubious Paradise of Apocalypse Now," *International Institute for Strategic Studies*, Vol. 57, No. 3, May 11, 2015, pp. 7–56. As of October 6, 2015:
https://www.iiss.org/en/publications/survival/sections/2015-1e95/survival--global-politics-and-strategy-june-july-2015-b48d/57-3-02-fromson-and-simon-02f4

Habib, Mustafa, "Tough Choices: Everyone Agrees, Shiite Militias Must Be Invited to Fight in Ramadi," Niquash.org, May 21, 2015. As of October 6, 2015:
http://www.niqash.org/en/articles/security/5013

Haddad, Fanar, *Sectarianism in Iraq: Antagonistic Visions of Unity*, New York: Columbia University Press, 2011, pp. 206–209.

International Institute of Strategic Studies, *The Military Balance 2016*, London: Routledge, 2016.

"Iraq Situation Report, August 12–13, 2015," Institute for the Study of War, August 13, 2015. As of October 6, 2015:
http://www.understandingwar.org/backgrounder/
iraq-situation-report-august-12-13-2015

Irish, John, "U.S. Says 10,000 Islamic State Militants Killed in Nine-Month Campaign," Reuters, June 3, 2015. As of October 6, 2015:
http://www.reuters.com/article/2015/06/03/
us-mideast-crisis-blinken-idUSKBN0OJ0I620150603

al-Kadhimi, Mustafa, "Could Saudi-Iraqi Ties Be Key to Defeating Islamic State?" Al Monitor.com, October 9, 2015. As of October 15, 2015:
http://www.al-monitor.com/pulse/originals/2015/10/iraq-saudi-arabia-relations-
extremism-isis-common-interests.html

Katzman, Kenneth, and Carla E. Humud, "Iraq: Politics and Governance," Congressional Research Service, September 16, 2015. As of October 6, 2015:
https://www.fas.org/sgp/crs/mideast/RS21968.pdf

Knights, Michael, "The Future of Iraq's Armed Forces," Baghdad, Iraq: Al-Bayan Center for Planning and Studies, March 2016. As of March 14, 2016:
http://www.bayancenter.org/en/wp-content/uploads/2016/03/The-future.pdf

Knights, Michael, "The Long Haul: Rebooting U.S. Security Cooperation in Iraq," Policy Focus 137, Washington Institute for Near-East Policy, January 2015. As of October 6, 2015:
http://www.washingtoninstitute.org/policy-analysis/view/
the-long-haul-rebooting-u.s.-security-cooperation-in-iraq

Lund, Aron, "Syria's Kurdish Army: An Interview with Redur Khalil," CarnegieEndowment.org, December 25, 2013. As of October 6, 2015:
http://carnegieendowment.org/syriaincrisis/?fa=54016

McCants, William, *The ISIS Apocalypse: The History, Strategy and Doomsday Vision of the Islamic State*, New York: St. Martin's Press, 2015.

Mueller, Karl P., Jeffrey Martini, and Thomas Hamilton, *Airpower Options for Syria: Assessing Objectives and Missions for Aerial Intervention*, Santa Monica, Calif.: RAND Corporation, RR-446-CMEPP, 2013. As of October 6, 2015:
http://www.rand.org/pubs/research_reports/RR446.html

Posen, Barry R., "Prelude to a Quagmire: The Addition of 450 New U.S. Military Trainers to Iraq Is the Next Step Down a Slippery Slope," *Foreign Policy*, June 16, 2015. As of October 6, 2015:
http://foreignpolicy.com/2015/06/16/prelude-to-a-quagmire-obama-iraq-isis/

Reuter, Christoph, "The Terror Strategist: Secret Files Reveal the Structure of Islamic State," *Spiegel*, April 18, 2015. As of October 6, 2015:
http://www.spiegel.de/international/world/islamic-state-files-show-structure-of-
islamist-terror-group-a-1029274.html

Robinson, Linda, *Tell Me How This Ends: General David Petraeus and the Search for a Way Out of Iraq*, New York, N.Y.: PublicAffairs Books, 2008.

Robinson, Linda, Patrick B. Johnston, and Gillian Oak, *U.S. Special Operations Forces in the Philippines, 2001–2014*, Santa Monica, Calif.: RAND Corporation, RR-1236-OSD, 2016. As of April 6, 2016:
http://www.rand.org/pubs/research_reports/RR1236.html

RT News, "Russia Deploys Cutting-Edge S-400 Air Defense System to Syrian Base After Su-24 Downing," November 26, 2015. As of March 19, 2016:
https://www.rt.com/news/323596-s400-russia-syria-airbase-turkey

Shear, Michael, Helene Cooper, and Eric Schmitt, "Obama Administration Ends Effort to Train Syrians to Combat ISIS," *New York Times*, October 9, 2015. As of October 15, 2015:
http://www.nytimes.com/2015/10/10/world/middleeast/pentagon-program-islamic-state-syria.html

Shiwesh, Ahmed, "U.S.-Trained Rebels Rejoin the Fight North Syria," Aranews.com, July 18, 2015. As of October 6, 2015:
http://aranews.net/2015/07/us-trained-rebels-rejoin-the-fight-north-syria

Smith, Alexander, "Iraqi PM Haider Al-Abadi Says Forces Lost 2,300 Humvees to ISIS," NBCNews.com, June 1, 2015. As of October 6, 2015:
http://www.nbcnews.com/storyline/isis-terror/
iraqi-prime-minister-haider-al-abadi-says-his-forces-lost-n367596

Sowell, Kirk H., "The Rise of Iraq's Militia State," CarnegieEndowment.org, April 23, 2015. As of October 6, 2015:
http://carnegieendowment.org/sada/?fa=59888

Special operations advisers, interviews with the author, five locations in Iraq, May 2015.

Stern, Jessica, and J. M. Berger, *ISIS: The State of Terror,* New York: Ecco, 2015.

"Strategic Framework Agreement for a Relationship of Friendship and Cooperation Between the United States of America and the Republic of Iraq," U.S. Department of State, November 17, 2008. As of October 15, 2015:
http://www.state.gov/documents/organization/122076.pdf

U.S. Department of Defense, "Operation Inherent Resolve: Targeted Operations Against ISIL Terrorists," March 15, 2016. As of March 24, 2016:
http://www.defense.gov/News/
Special-Reports/0814_Inherent-Resolve?source=GovDelivery

U.S. House of Representatives, Committee on Armed Services, "Hearing: U.S. Policy and Strategy in the Middle East," Washington, D.C.: Federal News Service, June 17, 2015a.

U.S. House of Representatives, Committee on Armed Services, "Hearing on U.S. Strategy for Syria and Iraq and its Implications for the Region," Washington, D.C., December 1, 2015b. As of March 28, 2016:
https://armedservices.house.gov/legislation/hearings/
us-strategy-syria-and-iraq-and-its-implications-region

———, "Hearing: World Wide Threats," Washington, D.C.: CQ Transcriptions, March 2, 2016.

U.S. House of Representatives, Committee on Foreign Affairs, "Hearing: From Iraq and Syria to Libya and Beyond: The Evolving ISIL Threat," Washington, D.C.: Federal News Service, February 10, 2016.

U.S. Senate, Committee on Armed Services, "Hearing: United States Central Command, Africa Command, and United States Special Operations Command," Washington, D.C.: Federal News Service, March 8, 2016.

Visser, Reidar, "Provincial Powers Law Revisions, Elections Results for Anbar and Nineveh: Is Iraq Headed for Complete Disintegration?" gulfanalysis.wordpress.com, June 27, 2013. As of October 15, 2015:
https://gulfanalysis.wordpress.com/2013/06/27/provincial-powers-law-revisions-elections-results-for-anbar-and-nineveh-is-iraq-headed-for-complete-disintegration

Weiss, Michael, and Hassan Hassan, *ISIS: Inside the Army of Terror,* New York: Regan Arts, 2015.